1. Saundersfoot
2. Harbour
3. Monkstone
4. Coppet Hall
5. Hean Castle
6. Woodside
7. Wisemans Bridge
8. Bonville's Court
9. Saundersfoot Station
10. Kilgetty Station
11. Begelly
12. Broom
13. Loveston
14. Templeton
15. Stepaside
16. The Grove
17. Heronsmill
18. Ludchurch
19. Blaencilgoed
20. Longstone
21. Lower Level
22. The Patches
23. Crickdam
24. Amroth
25. Amroth Castle
26. New Inn
27. Telpyn Point
28. Teague's Valley
29. Top Castle
30. Marros Sands
31. Ragwen
32. Morfabychan
33. Gilman Point
34. Pendine
35. Pendine Sands
36. Marros
37. Tremoilet
38. Swallowtree Bay
39. Beef's Park
40. Black Rock
41. Carmarthen Bay
42. Kilanow
43. Craig y borion
44. Duncow Hill
45. Garness
46. Jeffreston
47. Kingsmoor Common
48. Netherwood
49. Thomas Chapel
50. Penybont
51. Pwll
52. Merrixton
53. Devil's Den [Rosehill]

OLD SAUNDERSFOOT
FROM MONKSTONE
TO MARROS

When tholes were still in vogue

OLD SAUNDERSFOOT
FROM MONKSTONE
TO MARROS

ROSCOE HOWELLS

Gomer Press

To Mary Griffiths

Who has given so much over the years to the people of
an area she loves so well.

Where once we dwelt our name is heard no more,
Children not thine have trod my nursery floor;
And where the gard'ner Robin, day by day,
Drew me to school along the public way,
Delighted with my bauble coach, and wrapt
In scarlet mantle warm, and velvet capt,
'Tis now become a history little known.

WILLIAM COWPER
—On the Receipt of My Mother's Picture.

First Printed 1977
Second Edition 1987

© Gomer Press/Roscoe Howells

Published by
Gomer Press Ltd
Llandysul, Dyfed
Wales

Printed by
J. D. Lewis & Sons
Llandysul, Dyfed
Wales

Designed by
Roger Lloyd Jones

SBN 85088 423 3

Contents

List of illustrations
Acknowledgements
Foreword
Introduction
The story of coal 1
Bonvilles Court and the harbour 6
Stepaside and Wisemansbridge 34
Heronsmill 49
Saundersfoot 53
Amroth 97
Fairs 115
The submerged forest 119
Marros 121
Glossary of local dialect 126
Index 130

List of illustrations

Front Cover   The *Verbena* from the original water colour by A. Chappel of Goole.

Back cover   The invalid carriage of yesteryear

Frontispiece   When tholes were still in vogue

1   Coppet Hall early 1900's.
2   Coppet Hall sandbanks 1920's.
3   Coppet Hall sandbanks 1976.
4   Headstone in St. Issell's churchyard.
5   The Black Walk early 1900's.
6   The Black Walk 1976.
7   Remains of old mooring posts at Wisemansbridge.
8   Remains of coal tally office at Wisemansbridge.
9   Bonvilles Court colliery early 1900's.
10   C. Ranken Vickerman.
11   Hean Castle 1869. From a picture given to C. H. R. Vickerman by his mother on his 13th birthday.
12   Hean Castle 1976.
13   Railway Street with name of H. L. Read's shipyard top right hand corner.
14   *The Lady of the Isles* aground following a storm 1907.
15   East Anglian coal boats in Saundersfoot harbour 1870 including the 92-ton schooner the *Gleaner* of Woodbridge and the 86-ton schooner the *Harriet* of Ipswich.
16   Saundersfoot harbour c. 1900 with a load of pitprops brought in from Ireland.
17   Saundersfoot harbour 1908.
18   The *Bulldog* on the Thomas Chapel line.
19   The timbers at Coppet Hall exposed following storms in late 1950's.
20   The railway line to Stepaside.
21   A cliff fall on the Stepaside line 1921.
22   The 'middle' or 'short' tunnel.
23   The old Stepaside line 1976.
24   Old stone sleepers.
25   The Incline at Saundersfoot.
26   The *Rosalind*.
27   Drams linked by outside chains as well as couplings.
28   Bonville's Court colliery.
29   Bonville's Court colliery.
30   Bonville's Court colliery 1976.
31   Coal drams on the harbour weighbridge.
32   The Office on the harbour gutted by fire 1913.
33   The office staff 1921.
34   Pay day.
35   Homeward bound.
36   The 1895 Priestman oil engine from Bonville's Court colliery presented to the British Science Museum by J. F. Vickerman in 1926.
37   The *Bulldog* leaving Saundersfoot July 1939.
38   The *Bulldog*.
39   Loading coal Saundersfoot harbour 1937.
40   Loading coal Saundersfoot harbour.
41   The last years of Saundersfoot's coal trade.
42   Iron stack, made from boiler linings by William Daniel Evans, being raised into position 1927. The pit manager, J. C. Samuel, is in foreground.
43   The ostler's house, Bonville's Court cottage, with three stacks in background.
44   Charles Vickerman and his wife on a visit to Bonville's Court colliery.
45   Typical clom cottage.
46   Clom house St. Brides Hill, Saundersfoot 1920's.
47   The same house, 1976.
48   Business circular, 1892.
49   The chemist shop Saundersfoot.
50   Delivering beer along the sands to the pub at the back of the chemist shop.
51   The *Rosalind* outside the chemist stores.
52   Thos. Owen, clockmaker, outside his business premises in Railway Street, 1900.
53   The 'endless chain' by means of which Tom Roblin raised his sacks of flour.
54   A stonemason's mark on the Basin wall.
55   The Basin showing blacksmith's shop and weighbridge.
56   The same place 1976.
57   The blacksmith's shop on the harbour.
58   The sluice gates.

59 Charles Vickerman on Saundersfoot harbour with St. Issell's House in background.

60 The same place 1976.

61 The doss house alongside the old brewery, c. 1890.

62 The Burrows patch

63 Crickdam patch and remains of blacksmith's shop.

64 The boundary stone on the Cliff road.

65 The old stables at Amroth beneath the new bandstand, c. 1908.

66 Remains of the Grove casting shed, 1965.

67 The Grove caravan site, 1976.

68 'The Pan'.

69 The Cambrian, Stepaside, 1976.

70 Turnpike road milestone.

71 Turnpike road milestone.

72 Author's parents' wedding day. Ben Howells standing back row right. John Jones standing second from left.

73 Lay-by, 1976.

74 Grove pit Cornish beam engine shed, 1976.

75 Grove lime kilns, 1976.

76 'The Boers' on their way home outside the chemist stores, the collecting point for those who had called for a pint at the Globe.

77 'The Armour' outside the Office.

78 Jack Davies, Stepaside, at 94 years of age the only survivor of those who worked down the Lower Level, 1976.

79 Martha Richards who when she died at the age of 93 in 1974 was the last of the women to have worked in the Stepaside pits.

80 The Rosalind with the Stepaside men on their way through Railway Street to Bonville's Court colliery, 1909.

81 Kilgetty pit, Stepaside.

82 The Stack, Stepaside.

83 The Woodside foundry and brickworks in proximity to the railway line at Wisemansbridge c. 1920.

84 The same site, 1976.

85 The foundry in the 1920's.

86 The same site 1976.

87 Iron headstone in Sardis cemetery.

88 Foundry workers. Centre John David. Right Tom David. The boy, Frank David, was killed in World War I.

89 'New Alus' demolished in 1921.

90 Wisemansbridge Inn, c. 1903.

91 Wisemansbridge, c. 1900.

92 Section of O.S. original drawings, 1809-11.

93 Headstone Templeton Congregational cemetery.

94 Headstone Templeton Congregational cemetery.

95 The last remains of Heronsmill house, 1976.

96 The footbridge used before the ford was piped under the road.

97 The Den, 1976.

98 Four generations. Edmund Griffiths nursing g.-grandson Kenneth.

99 'Cap'n' Darby with a young summer visitor, 1929.

100 Miners digging coal on the beach during the strike in 1922.

101 Locals.

102 Ostler George Williams and pit pony Nancy.

103 Bertie Howells (left) and his men, 1927.

104 Bill Frost.

105 Author's grandmother, c. 1900.

106 Caldey shop, 1976.

107 Jack Childs.

108 Ted Goring.

109 Billy Williams on the Rosalind with David Darby and Ambrose Lilbourne (right).

110 Locals picking cockles during World War I.

111 Laugharne cockle-pickers at Saundersfoot.

112 Sgt. Nicholas.

113 P.C. Henton.

114 Sgt. William Evans and P.C. Anthony Thomas, 1907. P.C. Thomas eventually became Deputy Chief Constable of Pembrokeshire.

115 1976 same place.

116 Saundersfoot life-saving club, 1913.

117 Saundersfoot Volunteer Training Corps, 1915.

118 Peace Day 1918.

119 Saundersfoot sailing boats, 1904.

120 C. H. Vickerman's the Ranee, 1909.

121 Longshore sports and regatta, 1908.

122 Longshore sports and regatta, 1908.

123 Longshore sports and regatta, 1908.
124 Longshore sports and regatta, 1909.
125 Saundersfoot regatta early 1900's.
126 Regatta 1912.
127 A visiting competitor, the *Zinita* of Penarth, 1912.
128 The harbour, 1883.
129 The Front beach, c. 1898.
130 Harbour and Front beach 1976.
131 Jack Childs laying up his boat, the *Stella Maris*, formerly owned by the Benedictine monks of Caldey, c. 1928.
132 The harbour in the 1920's.
133 The harbour in the 1920's.
134 The harbour, 1976.
135 The harbour in the 1920's.
136 The harbour, c. 1944.
137 The harbour, 1976.
138 Saundersfoot sports.
139 Saundersfoot—cycle race in progress.
140 Saundersfoot sports.
141 France Fair 1920's.
142 Old foundations on Monkstone, 1976.
143 The Elephant's Trunk—an interestingly shaped rock between Swallow Tree Bay and Johnny's Grove.
144 Saundersfoot Rovers, 1921.
145 Saundersfoot A.F.C., c. 1929.
146 Kilgetty A.F.C., 1925.
147 Howard Prout leaves Bonville's Court colliery from the last shift, 1930.
148 Billy Griffiths with the F.A. Cup, 1927.
149 The tennis court Coppet Hall.
150 Saundersfoot male voice choir early 1920's. Author's father standing 8th from left.
151 Saundersfoot Boy Scouts, 1921.
152 Saundersfoot Girl Guides.
153 Cambrian Terrace, c. 1905.
154 Cambrian Terrace, c. 1905.
155 Cambrian Terrace, c. 1905.
156 Cambrian Terrace, 1976.
157 Roger Griffiths with one of the first motor-bikes to come into the village, 1914.
158 Stanley Scourfield with Saundersfoot's first delivery van.
159 William Beddoe Snr. in Milford Terrace, c. 1905.
160 Saundersfoot station, 1914.
161 Johnnie Ormond's first 'bus and the author's father's motor bike and sidecar.
162 Greens 'bus links up from Haverfordwest and Narberth.
163 Railway Street, c. 1906.
164 Railway Street early 1920's.
165 The Strand, 1976.
166 John Edwards water carrier.
167 The Glen and St. Brides Hill, 1904.
168 St. Brides Hotel, 1935.
169 Operation Jantzen 1943. Model of coastal area. U.S. Army photo.
170 Landing exercises on Front beach. U.S. Army photo.
171 Directing operations from the culvert at Coppet Hall. U.S. Army photo.
172 Bethany chapel, c. 1900.
173 The author's mother, c. 1901 (formerly Nelly Jones).
174 The Front beach, c. 1900.
175 The Front beach, 1976.
176 The Front beach, c. 1900.
177 The Front beach, 1976.
178 The village, c. 1890.
179 'Visiting celebrity' Kenneth Griffith deep in conversation with one of the older inhabitants, Osborne Evans, about their own families.
180 The chapel window at Amroth Castle. In good condition up to 1960 but badly damaged since.
181 Benjamin Rees—died 1870—who gave the land on which Ebenezer chapel was built.
182 Big Day carnival in the 1930's.
183 Amroth Castle, c. 1938.
184 The same site 1976.
185 Amroth, c. 1910.
186 Amroth, c. 1920.
187 Amroth, c. 1938.
188 Amroth, c. 1950.
189 Amroth, 1976.
190 Thomas Richards' sea wall.
191 The storms of 1931.

192 After the storm of 1931. The house was pulled down for the road to be built higher on the cliff.
193 The storms of the 1950's.
194 The storms of the 1950's.
195 After the storms.
196 After the storms.
197 The remains of Cliff Cottage.
198 New Inn 'lake' and Amroth Castle beach, 1902.
199 The same site 1976.
200 Lord Nelson commemorative plaque Amroth Castle.
201 Dick Absalom.
202 Extract from Amroth Parish Council minute book of 1901.
203 Saundersfoot village school c. 1927. Miss Maudie Simpson right. Author front row right.
204 Toll-gat post Cliff Road, 1976.
205 Amroth Seagulls 1920's.
206 Amroth Juniors, c. 1949.
207 Stepaside Fair, c. 1925.
208 Mrs. Attewell.
209 Some of the Danter family.
210 Danters' galloping horses.
211 Danters in the Cambrian hotel paddock Saundersfoot.
212 Remains of submerged forest at Marros 1976.
213 Remains of submerged forest at Marros 1976.
214 Remains of submerged forest at Marros 1976.
215 Walking sticks made from submerged forest remains at Amroth more than a century ago.
216 Top Castle overlooking Marros beach.
217 Bones of a *bos primigenius* dug up at Amroth in 1931 and given to the National Museum. This is believed to be the URUS referred to by Julius Caesar during his time in Germany but was probably extinct by the time of the Roman occupation of Britain.
218 Jim & Amy Mollison, 1933.
219 Remains of the *Rover* wrecked c. 1870's.
220 Wreck of the *Treviga*, 1923.
221 Tom & Jenny Morris in the 1870's.
222 Tom & Jenny Morris's headstone Pendine.
223 Prince Consort Memorial, Tenby.
224 Tom Harries the day he finished Marros war memorial, c. 1920. The original school is in the background.
225 Marros war memorial, 1976.

Acknowledgements

In collecting the pictures for this work I have had some marvellous and enthusiastic help from many people. Eventually it became a case of an embarrassment of riches and not knowing what to leave out. To thank all those who have helped would be impossible because they are so numerous. Therefore I cannot name a single one for fear of giving offence, however unintentionally, to others. In many cases I have been entrusted with treasured family possessions which their owners, I know, have refused to lend elsewhere.

It is impossible to express gratitude adequately to such a response as this just as it is impossible to put into words how heart-warming it has been to renew acquaintance with some I have not seen for too long and to experience again the warmth of their fellowship.

The one thing we all have in common is our love of the area which means so much to all of us. I can only hope they will not be disappointed in what I like to regard as a joint effort, because without their help it would not have been possible, and, in thanking them, express the additional hope that together we have produced something which will not only give pleasure to Saundersfooters wherever they may be but leave a useful record for Saundersfooters still to come.

If not quite a Saundersfooter, my old friend of boyhood, Kenneth Griffith, also has roots which go so deep into the soil of the area covered in these pages as to make him truly qualified to write a foreword to such a work. For the generous way in which he so readily agreed to do this I would also express my sincere thanks.

R.H.

Foreword

All that I have seen of Roscoe Howells' book is the 'first proof'—without the pictures to go with it.

I accepted the invitation to write this 'foreword' with alacrity and no sooner had I accepted than Roscoe bombarded me with admonitions such as: 'Look boy', (I am now 57 years old) 'I don't want any soft-soap like "this is a wonderful book"; I want you to write whatever you think!' Well, what I think is that the book (even without the pictures) is full of wonder for me. It is full of warm confirmation of almost lost memories of my childhood. While sitting close to a 'culm' fire (refer to Mr. Howells' text) as a little boy, at 'The Square' (my family's old home) at Stepaside, I can distantly recall talk of Loveston colliery, Swallow Tree Bay, Coppet Hall and 'Big Day' at Amroth. Yes, I have been to a 'Big Day' at Amroth! The place-names re-echo the vivid ghost memories of long long ago. I can remember the colliers walking between Kilgetty and Saundersfoot with black faces. I can remember the little railway. I can remember so much of the beauty and character that has now gone. And I thank Roscoe for conducting an aggressive campaign, over many years, to *keep* as much of the precious past as questionable progress married to pompous thick headed bureaucracy will allow.

The highpoint of the book for me? I will quote it: 'My stepmother's father, Jimmy Lloyd, was a forester on the Picton Estate, where he worked and was very friendly with Edmund Griffiths, one of the renowned stonemasons of the time . . .' Edmund Griffiths was my paternal Great Grandfather and I am so happy to be linked with his proud name in this book.

Wherever I may be and whatever work I am doing I have always endeavoured to emulate the standards set by my Great Grandfather and my beloved Grandfather, Ernest Griffiths, two 'renowned stonemasons'.

Kenneth Griffith, Tempest Films Limited,
1-6 Falconberg Court, London W1V 5FG,

Introduction

A picture, they say, is worth a thousand words. Certainly no words on their own could create a picture to show the change which has taken place in and around Saundersfoot during the last half century. To the modern visitor it is inconceivable that the port and its initial prosperity were built on coal, for in few places can the change since those comparatively recent times have been more complete or spectacular.

The purpose of this book is to tell as much as possible of the history of the area during the last hundred years or so from the pictures which are available and, in places, to show from present day pictures the transformation which has taken place, although, in many cases, years of vegetation or new buildings make this impossible.

The modern history of Saundersfoot cannot be told without reference to neighbouring villages. Just as it is true to say that you only have to scratch the skin of a townsman to find a countryman underneath, because of the exodus from the country to the town during the Industrial Revolution, so it is a fact that, as a result of the prosperity which coal once brought to Saundersfoot, most of the true natives of the village, and there are not many of them left, will trace their own descent to neighbouring villages such as Stepaside, Kilgetty, Amroth, Jeffreston, Martletwy and even Pendine beyond the far confines of Little England Beyond Wales.

Although I was born in Saundersfoot, my father was born in neighbouring Wisemansbridge, as were his father and grandfather before him, my mother was born in Cresselly and my stepmother in Kilgetty. Originally I had intended to write a book on the area telling something of its history as seen through these personal connections. But when I began to collect pictures to illustrate it I found myself with so many that the idea of the present work suggested itself.

There is no complete work on Saundersfoot and the surrounding area. In his book, *The Saundersfoot Story*, Thomas G. Stickings has collected much which is of value of the earlier history of the village, and M. R. C. Price has provided a thoroughly commendable and reliable history entitled *The Saundersfoot Railway* which also includes much useful detail of the coalmining and iron activities. Useful information concerning Saundersfoot can also be found in two excellent booklets based on original thesis, *The Coal Industry in Pembrokeshire* by George Edwards and *Pembrokeshire Sea-Trading Before 1900* by Barbara J. George. *Children in the Mines 1840-42* by R. M. Evans is another superior little publication well worth reading. The various glossy guides, designed to extract money from the unsuspecting tourists, may be safely ignored, lifted as they so often are from other sources which in some cases were themselves unreliable in the first place.

A lack of the necessary pictures must inevitably prevent a work such as this from telling the complete story, and no attempt will be made to repeat in any great detail that which has been quoted or written about, more or less adequately, elsewhere. There are, however, certain things which have been previously ignored, neglected or long forgotten, and it is hoped that, personal though some of them may be in their connections, they may yet be considered of sufficient interest for something more than a passing mention to have been justified.

The true history of any place, of course, is largely the story of its people, for people are life itself. Except where relevant, however, especially in group pictures, individuals have not been identified, the reasoning being that locals will recognise them anyway whilst visitors would not be particularly interested.

For the same reason, there has been no attempt to document pictures to the extent of elaborating on what buildings had or had not appeared at any given time. Again, locals will, with considerable interest, note these things for themselves.

Lastly, the occasional picture has been reproduced purely because it is in itself so evocative of an age that has gone. If it is claimed that a picture, however charming, of Tenby boatmen fashioning wooden tholes, has no place in these pages, then equally it may be argued that at some time or other they must have put into Saundersfoot. And there is now no one old enough either in Tenby or Saundersfoot to be able to identify them.

The overall aim, then, has been to produce a book which will mean something more than nostalgia to the native, be of interest, with maybe an element of surprise, to the visitor, and perhaps, without any pretensions to scholarship or claims of exhaustive research, be of some small value to the historian.

Above all, I hope it may prove to be not unworthy as a record of 'my own folks'.

There are two points which, since the publication of the first edition, need clarification.

On p29 the reference to the Great Western Railway is misleading. The railway which reached Saundersfoot in 1863 was the old Pembroke and Tenby Railway, with a link to Whitland in 1866. This line was not completely absorbed by the G.W.R. until 1897.

The other point which needs further mention is the reference on p97 to the Act of Union in 1834. This was, of course, the Poor Law Amendment Act under which the Unions came into being and not to be confused with the Act of Union of England and Wales in 1536 and 1542.

Three Pictures have come to light since the first edition was published. Although it is not possible for them to be reproduced in ideal positions alongside the text, it was felt that it would be a pity for them not to be included at all.

On p52 is a picture of Ben James and his sister Sarah, a legendary couple, who for many years kept the Wisemansbridge Inn.

A picture of the last boat being built on Saundersfoot harbour, probably somewhere in the 1860's, appears on p88, and the delightful extra picture on p118 is of a scene when corn was being threshed in the Cambrian hotel paddock.

The extra picture on p114 shows ten of the same group thirty-five years later on the occasion of the author's sixty-fifth birthday.

Lastly, in the introduction, I said that there was now no one old enough either in Tenby or Saundersfoot, to identify the two Tenby fishermen in the frontispiece. I was wrong. They were subsequently identified for me by the late Mr. Howard Nicholls as Tommy Goodridge (Chad) and Joe Wickland.

At eight o'clock on the Sunday morning of October 7th 1984, the village was shattered by an explosion which was heard and felt for miles around. It was caused by a leaking gas main and destroyed what the older generation have always known as Beddoe's Corner. The Cambrian Hotel was so badly damaged that, for some time, its future was in doubt, and there was colossal damage to property in the area.

When the children of today are old men and women they will tell their grand-children of the miracle by which no one was killed. Had the explosion occurred twenty-four hours later there would have been dozens of children waiting for the school buses and what would have been the resulting tragedy scarcely bears contemplation. A few weeks earlier at the same time the area would have been thronged with visitors.

The story of coal

'Saundersfoot is a flourishing little port, in the parish of St. Issells, about three miles N.E. from Tenby. It possesses a commodious harbour, well sheltered from the western winds, and connected by tramways with some extensive collieries, the coals from which are excellent, there is also an abundance of iron and limestone, altogether forming a favourable picture of future prosperity'.

Thus did Slater's Directory of 1868 refer to Saundersfoot. It is a reference which is all the more significant when it is realised that in that same year it was saying of Tenby, following a reference to the oyster trade, 'The chief support of the inhabitants in general is derived from the many visitors who frequent this place during the summer'.

Long before the building of Saundersfoot Harbour in 1829 and the completion of the first part of the railway in 1832, followed by the sinking of Bonvilles Court pit in 1846, coal was being mined in the area and exported from the open, sandy beaches of the bay.

There is a record of coal being mined near Saundersfoot early in the fourteenth century. By the sixteenth century the activity was considerable, much of the coal at that time being used for the burning of lime which was used to improve the land.

Acknowledged as being the best coal in the world, its great heating qualities and freedom from smoke became recognised much further afield and the demand in the seventeenth and eighteenth centuries was considerable. Working conditions, however, were primitive and consequently wasteful. Pits were sunk by driving in on a slope and the seam worked in all directions. Then, due to problems of flooding and lack of adequate ventilation, they would be abandoned. All over the area these uncharted workings of 'the old men', as they were known, remained as a hazard for later generations of miners and one such resulted in the Loveston colliery disaster of 1936.

Before the building of the harbour, coal was loaded into boats at Swallow Tree bay, where there was a lime kiln as well as pits, and it is said that it was from here the first load of Pembrokeshire coal was shipped to London. Limestone was brought to the kiln there and coal taken on the return voyage. By far the greater activity, however, was at Coppet Hall, to which beach coal was hauled by means of a track from pits in the area of the church. At the beginning of the nineteenth century the carts were being pulled down to the boats on the beach by the unusual combination of two oxen and two horses. For generations after the track had been abandoned the cinder surface remained and gave this popular footpath its name of the Black Walk. At that time the track ran along the side of a marsh which was reclaimed to make the present day Coppet Hall meadow in 1870 by filling in with refuse from the colliery and diverting the stream from the mill to a culvert which emerged on the beach. Following this the sandbanks were formed. Although erudite writing is to be found on the likely derivation of the name, Coppet Hall, it is thought locally to be a corruption of the original Coalpit haul, as a tombstone in St. Issells cemetery clearly indicates. A map of 1818 gives the name as Cupid's Hole but to point this out is perhaps to confuse the issue still further and to suggest that the scholars have much more research to do as yet.

There were similar pits at Amroth and Stepaside, and it was from these that coal was driven, in many cases in bullockdrawn carts, to Wisemansbridge for loading into fifty to sixty ton boats on the open beach. One of the coal yards was at Duncow Hill where my great grandfather, Richard Howells, lived and where my father was born.

It was a common practice, where practicable, to drain the water from some of these pits by means of adit levels, and, even in the driest weather, wet patches on the beaches remain as evidence of their continued existence.

1 Coppet Hall early 1900's.

2 Coppet Hall sandbanks 1920's.

3 Coppet Hall sandbanks 1976.

2

4   Headstone in St. Issell's churchyard.

5   The Black Walk early 1900's.

6   The Black Walk 1976.

3

Towards the end of the eighteenth century a canal was built by Lord Milford to transport coal from Stepaside to Wisemansbridge but this was an engineering failure and in fact was never completed. Richard Howells' father, George Howells, worked on this canal.

Conditions underground were deplorable with women and children harnessed like animals, in crawling and stooping positions, to haul the coal skips. Human life was expendable. My great grandmother worked in the New Hayes pit at Thomas Chapel as also did my great grandfather who was one of the boys interviewed by the Government inspectors in 1840-42.

In later years conditions improved with the women only being employed above ground on such tasks as riddling coal on the 'belt' or 'strap'. This was before the age of equal opportunity for the sexes.

7   **Remains of old mooring posts at Wisemansbridge.**

8   Remains of coal tally office at Wisemansbridge.

4

9   Bonvilles Court colliery early 1900's.

Bonvilles Court and the harbour

The leading industrialist and developer during the latter half of the nineteenth century was Charles Ranken Vickerman. His father, John Vickerman, who lived in Essex, was solicitor to Lord Milford and this is how the family's connection with Pembrokeshire began. Charles Ranken Vickerman was also a solicitor and lived in Essex until moving to Hean Castle, which he bought in 1869 and rebuilt, in the 1870's, with red sandstone brought into Saundersfoot harbour from Runcorn, in Cheshire, as ballast.

10   C. Ranken Vickerman.

11   Hean Castle 1869. From a picture given to
C. H. R. Vickerman by his mother on his 13th
birthday.

There was also a considerable ship-building industry, the two main shipwrights being H. L. Read and Francis Beddoe, who had their yards along what was then known as Railway Street. There was some relationship between them and when Francis Beddoe died in 1873 H. L. Read took over his business and named the boat he launched in 1877 *Francis Beddoe*. She met her end, in 1920, like so many other stout ships of sail, along Pendine sands, although the *Francis Beddoe* went aground in fog.

A ship remembered with particular affection was the *Lady of the Isles*, a forty-four ton dandy, built in Jersey (hence her name) in 1868 and brought to Saundersfoot in 1879 by H. L. Read who had come to the area from Reading. When he died at the age of forty-three his young widow and daughters operated the small shipping business before the boat was sold. One of the daughters, Eleanor, was later to marry Charles Ranken Vickerman's son, C. H. R. (Charles) Vickerman, who succeeded his father in the business.

Before going down to Combe Martin to end her days the *Lady of the Isles* was owned and skippered during her last years in Saundersfoot by John Davies, better known as 'Cap'n Jack'. Jim Dunn sailed in her for thirteen years. One of her companions was the *Woodcock*, skippered by David Darby.

One of the finest of the Saundersfoot boats was the ninety-three ton ketch, *Verbena*, owned and skippered by Captain Graham who also owned the *Advance*.

12   Hean Castle 1976.

13 Railway Street with name of H. L. Read's
shipyard top right hand corner.

14 *The Lady of the Isles* aground following a storm
1907.

In addition to these local boats, however, there were many fine ketches and schooners which plied regularly to and from other ports, particularly in Kent and East Anglia, where the Saundersfoot anthracite was in great demand for malting at such places as Snape and Mistley, and many cargoes went to Ireland to Guinness in Dublin for the same purpose. Considerable quantities of anthracite also went abroad.

On the question of the high quality of the Saundersfoot anthracite, it was a cause for pride when it was used on the Royal Yacht, and Queen Victoria was so impressed with its smoke-free qualities that she thereafter insisted that no other coal should be used when she was on board.

15 East Anglian coal boats in Saundersfoot harbour 1870 including the 92-ton schooner the *Gleaner* of Woodbridge and the 86-ton schooner the *Harriet* of Ipswich.

16 Saundersfoot harbour c. 1900 with a load of pitprops brought in from Ireland.

9

The Saundersfoot railway, built in conjunction with the harbour, originally consisted of a line from Bonvilles Court to Thomas Chapel and a line to the harbour. The coal trams were at that time hauled by horses. Some ten years or more later a further line was added via Wisemansbridge to Stepaside. This passed the end of the old line at Coppet Hall, and required banking to traverse the marshy ground, and three tunnels before taking it along an embankment at the foot of the cliffs to Wisemansbridge. More than a century later, in the late 1950's, heavy storms exposed the timbers which had been used for the barrier facing, to keep back the sand from this new line, and it was following this that the sandbanks were formed.

17   Saundersfoot harbour 1908.

18   The *Bulldog* on the Thomas Chapel line.

19   The timbers at Coppet Hall exposed following
     storms in late 1950's.

20   The railway line to Stepaside.

21   A cliff fall on the Stepaside line 1921.

22   The 'middle' or 'short' tunnel.

23   The old Stepaside line 1976.

Up to this time the rails were held by 'chairs' bolted
into stone sleepers but in the 1870's the line was relaid
with heavier rails spiked into wooden sleepers and a
small steam engine introduced. She was subsequently
named the *Rosalind,* after Miss Rosalind Vickerman,
and ran from Stepaside to the harbour and to
Bonville's Court as far as the Incline. This was a
particular feature of the Saundersfoot line, with a
steep gradient, where the laden drams descended
from the top and hauled the empty drams up by their
impetus. The occasional breakaway dram and near
fatality eventually resulted in the evolving of a safer
linkage system with outside chains as well as the usual
coupling.

24   Old stone sleepers.

25   The Incline at Saundersfoot.

14

26   The *Rosalind*.

27   Drams linked by outside chains as well as
      couplings.

Until 1915 the laden drams were hauled from Bonvilles Court to the top of the Incline by horses but, in 1915, the *Bulldog,* another well-known little engine, was introduced. She worked above the Incline, running as far as Thomas Chapel until that line was closed in the 1920's, and then continued working from the top of the Incline to the pit until the closure of Bonville's Court in 1930.

Although, for the whole of its existence, the Saundersfoot railway confined its activities to the use of goods wagons, it did in fact have the distinction of operating one passenger vehicle in the form of a converted coal dram which the Vickerman family had for their personal use.

28   Bonville's Court colliery.

29 Bonville's Court colliery.

30 Bonville's Court colliery 1976.

17

31   Coal drams on the harbour weighbridge.

32   The Office on the harbour gutted by fire 1913.

33   The office staff 1921.

34   Pay day.

35 Homeward bound.

36 The 1895 Priestman oil engine from Bonville's
Court colliery presented to the British Science
Museum by J. F. Vickerman in 1926.

37　The *Bulldog* leaving Saundersfoot July 1939.

38　The *Bulldog*.

39 Loading coal Saundersfoot harbour 1937.

40 Loading coal Saundersfoot harbour.

For a time after the closure of Bonvilles Court culm continued to be driven from the tip, and also from other pits in the area which were all in their death throes, and lorries drove some coal to Saundersfoot harbour after the *Rosalind* had ceased to run. Although steam ships for some time had become part of the picture, smaller ketches, such as the *Mary Jane Lewis* and *The Cornish Lass,* continued to call until Bonville's Court closed and they carried loads of culm round the coast.

There have been many references to culm in writings on Pembrokeshire and the footnotes invariably give the meaning as 'small coal'. Whilst this is true to some extent it is a term which can be misleading to those who are not familiar with it. Small coal, of course, consists of beans and nuts which have not passed through the different grades of the riddle. Culm is the discarded remainder and consists also of anything which has been knocked about in handling, when the shot is fired, or shed and crushed under the dram wheels, and is subsequently 'clen up' as an old Pembrokeshire collier would have said. Culm, then, strictly speaking, is much smaller than small coal being no bigger than granulated sugar.

A particular type of culm was known as 'slash', but this was mined as such. The seam at Wood Level in Stepaside, for example, consisted only of slash. It was approached both by a pit and by a level and, such was its composition, it was possible for a man to shovel all day without knowing that he had been there any more than if he had been shoveling sand.

THE HARBOUR, SAUNDERSFOOT. 11144

41   The last years of Saundersfoot's coal trade.

42 Iron stack, made from boiler linings by William Daniel Evans, being raised into position 1927. The pit manager, J. C. Samuel, is in foreground.

43 The ostler's house, Bonville's Court cottage, with three stacks in background.

45 Typical clom cottage.

44 Charles Vickerman and his wife on a visit to Bonville's Court colliery.

Culm was, for generations, the traditional firing in Pembrokeshire cottages. Mixed with clay, or slime from the beach, it had water added and was made up into 'balls'. The fire was then 'stummed' down overnight and one or two holes inserted for ventilation. A poker eased into it in the morning would see the flame shooting up and a good heat would be given out. Indeed, it was this round-the-clock, all-the-year-round heat which alone made it possible for people to live in the lime-washed 'clom' houses which were made of a mixture of rubble, or even straw or brambles, and thick mud or clay. Without this constant heat the walls became damp and crumbled. With the advent of planning authorities and improvement grants it became impermissible to modernise this type of structure and clom dwellings passed into history.

Much of the clay used for making balls in the area was dug on Kingsmoor Common where the many holes and pits remain to tell their own story.

Although the harbour was built for the coal trade this was not the exclusive purpose for which it was used. The *Lady of the Isles,* amongst others, for many years carried general cargoes for Tom Roblin, 'Griffiths the chemist' and Mrs. Morris of Jubilee House. Such cargoes would include soap, oil cake, sugar, beer, fertiliser and groceries and paraffin for shops as far afield as Amroth, Jeffreston and Cresselly.

46   Clom house St. Brides Hill, Saundersfoot 1920's.

47   The same house, 1976.

25

A. D. Griffiths took over the general business at 'the chemist' from Thomas Mathias, father of Bentley Mathias who became something of a legend in the county's legal circles. The business ranged from dispensing medicine for humans and livestock through a bewildering combination which included a pub (the Globe) at the back, wines and spirits, cattle cake, seeds mixtures, fertiliser, insurance, a sub-branch of the Midland Bank, ships' chandlery, china and glass and, of course, sundries. Worthy of note in this context is the fact that he also employed Billy Morris who, before the first World War, used his great plate camera on its tripod and with its black cloth to record so much of the Saundersfoot of that time.

SAUNDERSFOOT,

October, 1892.

In issuing this circular, I beg to thank my numerous supporters and patrons for the generous support accorded me in the past, and trust that by supplying the best of everything the markets can afford at a fair remuneration, and paying prompt attention to all orders, to merit a continuance of the same.

Owing to the present state of my health, and the care and attention needed to carry on the business, I beg to inform you that I have engaged a qualified Chemist (Mr. ARTHUR GRIFFITHS) to assist me in carrying on the business.

The Drug Department will have his special attention. All Prescriptions, Family and Veterinary Recipes, will be carefully and accurately dispensed, with promptitude and the best of Drugs, and the experience he has had in London and the country will enable him to appeal with confidence for the patronage of the neighbourhood.

The other departments of the business will be carried on as heretofore, and the former standard of excellence maintained.

Hoping to be favoured with your further support,

I am, yours faithfully,

T. MATHIAS.

48   Business circular, 1892.

49   The chemist shop Saundersfoot.

50   Delivering beer along the sands to the pub at the
back of the chemist shop.

51   The *Rosalind* outside the chemist stores.

52   Thos. Owen, clockmaker, outside his business
premises in Railway Street, 1900.

oth Tom Roblin, who operated his hand-turned offee mill until well into the present century, and Mrs. Morris at Jubilee House, were shopkeepers in the great tradition of a long-forgotten age. Tom Roblin had two notches on his mahogany counter for measuring an ounce of twist. To the end, when he died in the 1920's, he remained loyal to the sea traders, but eventually the Great Western Railway, which had reached the Saundersfoot neighbourhood in 1863, won the battle by means of fierce price-cutting. When all competition by sea had been eliminated they increased their rates by a hundred per cent.

If the Incline was the special feature of the railway, the Basin was a not unimportant feature of the harbour. Here the stream, the fording of which possibly gave Saundersfoot its name in earlier centuries, was ponded back for the sluice gates to be opened at low water to clear the sandbank at the pier head and keep the bed of the harbour clear. On the basin wall it is still possible to see the marks of the stone masons on individual stones. It was done at a time when men took a pride in their work and possibly, since the marks appear in series, worked on a piece-work basis.

53   The 'endless chain' by means of which Tom Roblin raised his sacks of flour.

54   A stonemason's mark on the Basin wall.

55   The Basin showing blacksmith's shop and
weighbridge.

56   The same place 1976.

30

Another possible derivation of the name Saundersfoot, and popular when I was a boy, was that a family by the name of Saunders or Sanders had come over with William the Conqueror and they gave the place its name as the first place where they set foot.
The Sanders family did not in fact appear on the scene in the area until much later but, if they did come over with William and land on the English coast, Saundersfoot could have been the first place where they later set foot in Wales.

As a solicitor in London, before he came to Hean Castle, C. R. Vickerman had spent more of his time hunting the country round his estate at Thoby Priory, near Mountnessing in Essex, than he did in his London office. His same interest continued when he came to Pembrokeshire, with laying out a splendid cricket ground at Hean Castle and running his own team, and by the time of his death in 1897 his fortunes had already begun to wane.

In his last will and testament, drawn up in 1883, he had settled £10,000, the equivalent of more than half a million pounds at today's (1977) values, on his daughter Rosalind, but, in a codicil added in January 1893, he stated that 'whereas owing to the serious depreciation in the value of the land since the date of my Will and for other reasons it may be inconvenient to my son to pay or provide for the provision made by my Will for my daughter immediately or soon after my decease . . .'

The sequel to this was that Hean Castle and much of the estate was sold in 1899 to Sir William Thomas Lewis, who subsequently became the first Lord Merthyr. In that same year Charles Vickerman married Eleanor Read, a daughter of Henry Lewis (or variously Harry Louis) Read and a sister to 'Reggie' Read who was subsequently for many years the village postmaster. The Vickermans made their home at St. Issell's House, a handsome residence on Saundersfoot harbour, but later moved to live on St. Brides Hill because of trouble with the drains, as a result of which their two young sons were constantly ill with sore throats, and St. Issell's House stood empty for many years. At that time, such a sewerage scheme as there was in the village discharged direct into the Basin within easy smelling distance of St. Issell's House and continued in existence until the 1960's.

The agent to the Bonville's Court Coal Company was Edmund J. Harvey, a nephew to C. R. Vickerman, but, by the time the pit closed in 1930, the only directors were Mr. and Mrs. C. H. R. Vickerman and their son, John F. (Jack) Vickerman. The pit closed on April 17th, 1930 when, out of the three hundred men employed there, only forty were retained for a time for dismantling.

57   The blacksmith's shop on the harbour.

58   The sluice gates.

59 Charles Vickerman on Saundersfoot harbour
with St. Issell's House in background.

60 The same place 1976.

Apart from any feeling of antagonism to Ranken Vickerman as an employer, as evident from local newspaper reports of the time, as well as from the recollections of older people, the report of the Royal Commission on Land of 1893 shows him to have left something to be desired as a landlord. Typical of the era, only one tenant farmer dared to give evidence against him to the Commission and that was John Hilling who had been evicted from his smallholding because his father had sunk a small opencast pit of his own on someonelse's land. And he had only done this to try to earn money somehow because of his unsatisfactory situation as a tenant after he had spent his life improving his little farm and house and buildings.

The Rev. George Bancroft, who was appointed Minister of Bethesda in 1864, and who founded the Bethany in Saundersfoot in 1867, was a great worker for the poorer people and he gave evidence in a very courageous manner for those who were afraid to speak for themselves as well as testifying how a number of widows had been evicted in 1871 when other land was added to the Hean Castle estate. The general idea was that they were evicted merely because they had no vote.

Long before the closing of Bonvilles Court, ever since the 1870's, Saundersfoot had been attracting increasing numbers of summer visitors. By 1895 the newly formed St. Issell's Parish Council were advertising the advantages of the place in *Tit Bits* and starting in their attempts to close down the old 'doss house', alongside the brewery, where twenty tramps could put up for the night, on the grounds that their presence in the village was detrimental to the interests of the visitors and those who catered for them.

61   The doss house alongside the old brewery, c. 1890.

Stepaside and Wisemansbridge

From various points beneath the cliffs along the bay iron ore was dug and perhaps the scene of the greatest activity was eventually at the 'patches' between Wisemansbridge and Amroth. There had been considerable digging for iron ore, however, all along the cliffs of the bay. When my father was building a house in Saundersfoot for Dr. Hunter-Dunn (father of Joan who was later to be immortalised by poet John Betjeman), in the field beyond the Drill Hall in the 1930's, he had considerable trouble with the foundations as a result of subsidence caused by the old iron ore workings in the cliff along what was originally known as Railway Street but has now been so charmingly renamed the Strand. This working, and that in the cliffs between Saundersfoot and Wisemansbridge, met with some problems after the **building of the railway.**

The iron ore from Wisemansbridge is mostly associated with the ironworks opened at the Grove in the 1840's but, long before that, iron ore had been exported to Pembrey, where the harbour was built in 1810, until the failure of Thomas Gaunt's iron company of that name, the effects of which were sold in 1840. The company, however, had certainly ceased to operate as early as 1833. The iron ore dug at the patches was loaded into open boats, which were beached on the sand, by men and women carrying bags on their shoulders, up a plank at one side of the boat, across a plank, tipping the bag as they went, and then down a plank at the other side of the boat.

It was partly in order to develop this source of wealth in the vicinity that the Grove ironworks was opened **and** there followed a period of much activity.

62   The Burrows patch

here were four main patches between
Wisemansbridge and Amroth consisting of the Bridge
patch, nearest to Wisemansbridge, followed by
Lloyds or Rooksnest patch, then Crickdam and,
finally, the Burrows patch nearest to Amroth where
Cliff Cottage used to stand until it was washed away
by the sea. Lloyds patch took its name from the owner
of adjoining land, the boundary of which was marked
by a stone on the old cliff road bearing the initials
W L L. These initials stood for William Lloyd who
lived at the Laques at Llanstephan and was a
substantial property owner in West Wales. The old
stone is still there (1977). Its significance was passed
on to the younger generation by the late Bob John,
born very near to the spot at nearby White Leys,
father of my inseparable schoolday's mate of the same
name, and who, like my grandfather, as will be
mentioned later, considered himself lucky to get a
job on the road when the pit closed.

The term patch, often found in old legal documents
in the phrase 'piece or patch of land', was here used as
an equivalent to a plot or allotment of mineral
ground.

The individual patches were about twenty yards apart
and were usually worked by two men in each patch
who filled the rubbish, formerly into wheelbarrows
but later into wooden trams, then ran it over rails out
to the tip and tipped it onto the beach about fifty feet
below. All the iron ore known as 'mine', found during
the filling, was picked out and stocked in large beds or
piles, 2′ 6″ in height, outside the patch. The payment
of 9s 6d per ton for the iron ore during the winter was
based on a measurement system of $22\frac{1}{2}$ cubic feet to
the ton (equal to a square of iron ore or mine
3 ft x 3 ft x $2\frac{1}{2}$ ft). In the summer, when the tides
would allow the making of a road on the beach, the
whole of the winter stocked ore, after all slate or shale

63 Crickdam patch and remains of blacksmith's
shop.

64 The boundary stone on the Cliff road.

had been 'polled' off by women called 'pollers', was carted away to Stepaside and weighed. The difference between the actual weight was then adjusted and payment settled, usually with a few pounds coming to the workmen as a result of underestimating originally.

When the spring tides carried away the tips which consisted of anything between five and ten thousand tons of rubbish, a large quantity of clearly washed iron ore was strewn all over the beach and this was generally picked by women and children called 'mine pickers' and stocked in beds or small piles of two to three tons on the side of the cliffs, from which, when the tides suited, it was carted away to Stepaside as soon as there was a cartload in stock, the rates of payment being by actual weight at the same rate of 9s 6d per ton as for the iron ore from the patches above the beach.

Some of the horses used for haulage were kept in stables on top of which the old bandstand at Amroth

was subsequently built, but much of the carting was done on a freelance basis by farmers in the area. Throughout the summer the farmers would drive loads of ore to Stepaside and, having deposited this at the furnaces, would then load up with culm at the Grove pit and drive it to Blaencilgoed lime-kilns to exchange it for loads of lime for their land. It was, of course, a time when the coming of the railway had opened up new markets in the industrial areas of South Wales and there was every inducement to farm productively.

The quarries and lime-kilns were in full production at Ludchurch and Blaencilgoed at that time and on pay night the quarry workers would come down to 'The Pan', as the Miners Arms was known, at Stepaside, ready to do battle with the Stepaside colliers on a scale which, if the old timers are to be believed, would have made today's football hooligans look like velvet suited mamma's darlings drinking lemonade at the Sunday school party.

65   The old stables at Amroth beneath the new bandstand, c. 1908.

artly due to shortage of capital the Grove iron
nterprise went through some very difficult periods
nd was more than once 'on stop' before finally
osing down in 1877. Work had ceased on the
Visemansbridge to Amroth patches in the summer of
876. In 1851 there had been people living at
rickdam and the remains of the old blacksmith's
hop can still be seen. Near to this there was a large
nine yard'.

During the periods when there was no intake of iron
ore at the Grove, work at the patches had continued
and the ore was exported to Port Talbot. Much of this
now went from Saundersfoot harbour but some of it
was still loaded into open boats on the beach as in
former times. There was a big export trade round
about 1861 and Richard Howells, who died in 1864,
was particularly active in it. The men were paid a
shilling a day and the women sixpence.

66   Remains of the Grove casting shed, 1965.

67　The Grove caravan site, 1976.

68　'The Pan'.

69　The Cambrian, Stepaside, 1976.

38

Before moving to Duncow Hill in the 1850's Richard Howells had lived at the Cambrian, a mile or two up the road from Stepaside, just below the turning from the main road to Amroth and Wisemansbridge. Working on his own account as a coalminer and haulier he drove the stones to make the section of the road from Begelly cross to the county boundary at Castle Ely bridge, when the new road was built 'to improve the approaches to Pembroke Dock harbour' in 1837. He had a licence, mainly for supplying beer to the men working for him on the road, and some of the census returns and other records show him described occasionally as Inn Keeper and the Cambrian referred to variously as Cambrian Inn or Cambrian Mailway. When he left there the licence lapsed and the name was transferred about 1870 to what had previously been the Milford Arms in Saundersfoot. My father rebuilt the Cambrian as a pair of semi-detached houses about 1930.

Richard's son, Ben Howells, also later put his money into the development of a small pit at Stepaside, but he cut into one of the abandoned workings left by the 'old men' and, whilst he was no doubt lucky to come out of it with his life, he was consequently unfortunate enough to come out minus his money. He kept on his smallholding, so typical of the area, and went to work down the Lower Level. When that pit closed in 1900 he became a 'highway labourer', which was the term in which his death certificate referred to a roadman. By one of those odd twists of fate his 'length' was a three mile section of the road his father had built, from the Bont to Begelly Cross, with the turnpike milestones showing the distance as eleven miles and fourteen miles respectively to Hobbs Point. And in those days his duties also included breaking the stones and wheeling them in his wheelbarrow to mend the potholes in the days before tarmac. In those days, too, a roadman's length was something in which he took a great pride, with the gutters being kept clear, so that no water could damage the road surface, and the hedges and grass verges being a joy to behold. Today, no individual roadman is answerable for his own length and the country roads are neglected by sporadic gangs who are sent by central authority to lurch from one disorganised emergency to another.

70   Turnpike road milestone.

71   Turnpike road milestone.

72 Author's parents' wedding day. Ben Howells
standing back row right. John Jones standing
second from left.

73 Lay-by, 1976.

The Grove ironworks having been opened in the 1840's, a pit to supply it with coal was sunk on the hillside above. Later there was a row of lime kilns, two blast furnaces with blowing engines, coke ovens and a foundry. Advantage was taken of the slope behind the works to charge the blast furnaces from the higher ground. A railway line with a self-action incline brought the coal down to Stepaside valley and the coal trams were used to take the iron to Saundersfoot harbour for export.

The Grove pit closed in 1873 and the Lower Level further up the valley was sunk to replace it. The Grove continued to work for a year or two until the lower workings became flooded. A road underground connected the two pits and, for some years, for the convenience of the Grove ironworks, some coal from the Lower Level was actually landed from the Grove pit. There were, however, considerable ventilation problems at the Lower Level and, in the absence of a fan, a large fire, erected on a 'crampass' (a stand on iron legs), was made at the bottom of the Grove shaft and this had the effect of drawing the stale air down from the Lower Level and improving circulation. When the Lower Level closed in 1900 many of the men employed there went to work at Bonville's Court and were transported to and from work in coal drams pulled by the *Rosalind*. From that time she seems to have become affectionately known as the *Armour*. The Boer War was on in South Africa at the time and, somewhere out there, armoured trains which were much larger versions of the *Rosalind* had become quite famous. The Stepaside colliers became known in Saundersfoot as the Boers. Probably the name *Armour* for the *Rosalind* was derived from the same source.

In recent years it has frequently been stated that the *Rosalind* and her passengers were known as the 'Miners Express'. And this is nonsense. Never, as a boy in the village, did I ever hear the term, and never have I met a collier who ever used it or recalls it having been used.

74 Grove pit Cornish beam engine shed, 1976.

75 Grove lime kilns, 1976.

76 'The Boers' on their way home outside the chemist stores, the collecting point for those who had called for a pint at the Globe.

77 'The Armour' outside the Office.

The term originated on an occasion when a picture was being taken, and, in those early days of photography, the taking of a picture was an event of some importance when the whole street turned out to stand to attention. On this particular occasion some wag picked up a paint brush and a pot of white paint standing nearby and daubed the words Miners Express on one of the drams. Hence its use on many of the postcards of the day but it was never used elsewhere.

The *Rosalind* was housed at Stepaside and, when the Grove ironworks closed, some of the buildings were retained for use as workshops.

The Kilgetty pit at Stepaside was opened in the 1930's but only operated for a few years and was closed in 1939.

78 Jack Davies, Stepaside, at 94 years of age the only survivor of those who worked down the Lower Level, 1976.

79 Martha Richards who when she died at the age of 93 in 1974 was the last of the women to have worked in the Stepaside pits.

80 The *Rosalind* with the Stepaside men on their
way through Railway Street to Bonville's Court
colliery, 1909.

81 Kilgetty pit, Stepaside.

82 The Stack, Stepaside.

earer to Saundersfoot, and near Wisemansbridge, t the bottom of the hill below Hean Castle, a rickworks making the highest quality firebricks from he black clay underlying the coal seams was started t Woodside in the middle of the last century by 'homas Stokes of Hean Castle. Shortly afterwards, in 850, a family by the name of David opened the oundry nearby and this turned out a variety of roducts, including iron headstones, until it closed own, still in the ownership of the same family, in he 1920's.

The year 1921 also saw the end of New Alus (New Alehouse), at the bottom of Duncow Hill field, the garden of which had been in the Howells family for many years. It left only the Wisemansbridge Inn to supply what by this time had become only the very meagre alcoholic needs of the resident population when New Alus was pulled down and a new house built in its place.

83   The Woodside foundry and brickworks in proximity to the railway line at Wisemansbridge c. 1920.

84   The same site, 1976.

87 Iron headstone in Sardis cemetery.

85 The foundry in the 1920's.

86 The same site 1976.

88   Foundry workers. Centre John David.
Right Tom David. The boy, Frank David, was
killed in World War I.

89   'New Alus' demolished in 1921.

90   Wisemansbridge Inn, c. 1903.

91   Wisemansbridge, c. 1900.

Heronsmill

Heronsmill was a hamlet a mile or two inland from Stepaside and further up the valley than the Lower Level pit. The last map on which it appeared was that based on the Ordnance Survey original drawings of 1809-11 when it was shown as Herrings Mill. Later estate papers show it as Heirons Mill and finally Heronsmill.

The children of the area had a rhyme on the names of the various holdings:

Heronsmill, Underfoot Hill, Devil's Den and the Gangrel, Brandy Back, Pelecwm Stack, Rushyland and Rollin.

There was more to it which I cannot now remember.

Only the Den is now standing and that, in earlier maps, is given as Rosehill.

In its heyday, the hamlet could boast of one of just about every trade from miller to blacksmith and clogmaker to saddler. The miller was Walter Evans who had twenty donkeys which he used for carrying panniers to collect and deliver corn. He was a very fine gardener and did a great deal of grafting of pear and plum trees, some of which continued to bear fruit until comparatively recent times.

Walter Evans had 'married in' to Heronsmill, his wife being a daughter of Thomas Morris, who was a blacksmith.

92   Section of O.S. original drawings, 1809-11.

The coming of the railway, however, revolutionised the way of life in the rural areas and depression finally sounded the death knell for many such hamlet as that which clustered round Heronsmill. In the 1870's, before the closure of the Grove ironworks and the last days of the Grove pit, Walter Evans left Heronsmill. The leat to his mill is now completely silted up and, covered by dense growth, beyond the reach of camera, whilst only a few stones of the house remain beneath the great sycamore tree.

My stepmother's mother was one of the sixteen children of Walter Evans which is why I know so much of the unrecorded history of the quiet little backwater.

Her father, Jimmy Lloyd, was a forester on the Picton Estate, where he worked and was very friendly with Edmund Griffiths, one of the renowned stonemasons of his time. Edmund Griffiths, in fact, built the estate house for him when he married Ann Evans of Heronsmill.

93   Headstone Templeton Congregational cemetery.

94   Headstone Templeton Congregational cemetery.

95 The last remains of Heronsmill house, 1976.

96 The footbridge used before the ford was piped
under the road.

97 The Den, 1976.

Keepers of the Wiseman's Bridge Inn, Ben James and his sister Sarah.

98 Four generations. Edmund Griffiths nursing
g.-grandson Kenneth.

Saundersfoot

The children's rhyming conundrum was,

'Why did Templeton Kilgetty?
Because it trod on Saundersfoot.
Why did it tread on Saundersfoot?
Because it wouldn't Stepaside'.

There was, of course, particularly because of the coal mining and the harbour, an interdependence between Saundersfoot and the smaller surrounding villages so that, before going too far along the coast, it would perhaps be as well to complete the references to Saundersfoot at this stage.

As the result of two world wars, and the impact of motorised transport, this century has seen a tremendous change in the make-up of the rural population and nowhere could this have been much more evident than in the case of Saundersfoot. Apart from servicemen going away and bringing wives back with them, or servicemen being stationed in the area marrying local girls and subsequently settling in an area which appealed to so many of them, there has been the influx of people getting to know the area as holidaymakers and deciding to live there on retirement. Some of these people can trace their connections back for many years to their first

99 'Cap'n' Darby with a young summer visitor, 1929.

childhood visits when they became almost a part of the community. The village people, too, knew who would be coming to which houses and looked forward to the renewing of old friendships.

After the first war things began to change considerably and perhaps set a pattern which has developed since, but there were still many characters about with roots going far back into an age which has now gone for ever. As always, there was great poverty to be met with and this had assumed awful proportions by the time of the General Strike in 1926. Men hung about in desultory fashion, sitting on the Office wall (now the Barbecue) and focal point of village exchanges of news and gossip, "Vickerman's ponies" were brought up from the pit to graze in the field at the bottom of our garden, and an air of terrible gloom and despondency impinged itself even on young minds. My father was a builder employing maybe a dozen men and it was a harrowing experience to see grown men, with tears in their eyes, knocking on the door asking for work which was not to be had.

It should be said, too, that times were just as hard for the self-employed. The three builders in the village spent much of their time tendering against each other and outside builders, cutting their own throats very often, as well as each other's, in an almost hopeless attempt sometimes, to get what little work there was going.

Over the hedge from us when we moved up to St. Brides Hill there lived an old man by the name of Bill Frost. He was the founder and conductor of Saundersfoot Male Voice Choir and a deacon at the Bethany chapel where my mother had been a Sunday School teacher. A carpenter by trade Bill Frost, in 1895, patented an aeroplane. It was a dozen years before Alberto Santos-Dumont, the world-famous aeronautical inventor, achieved the first fluttering hopes from the ground in a power-driven machine in 1906, and fifteen years before an authentic flight in a man-carrying aeroplane equipped with an engine was made by Orville Wright at Dayton, Ohio.

100   Miners digging coal on the beach during the strike in 1922.

54

101   Locals.

102   Ostler George Williams and pit pony Nancy.

Although he has never been credited with it in what little has ever been written on the subject, I remember, when I was a boy, Bill Frost telling my father that he did make an attempt and the 'plane actually took to the air only to catch in the top of a tree as he tried to clear the hedge. It was fitted with a hydrogen cylinder on top and a crank onto a propellor. Before he could repair the damage a violent storm in the night carried the plane into the air and smashed it to pieces. Bill Frost broke his heart over this calamity but offered his patent to the Secretary of State for War. He had a reply from the Under Secretary, Mr. St. John Brodrick, who thanked Mr. Frost, as such characters unfailingly do, but went on to say, 'The nation does not intend to adopt aerial navigation as a means of warfare'. The remarkable old man, by now blind, died a virtual pauper in 1935 at the age of eighty-seven.

Amongst the old characters were many of those with earlier connections with the harbour and the old sailing ships, including 'Cap'n Jack', owner of the *Lady of the Isles*, who in later years kept the shop in Brewery Terrace. Prior to this the shop had been kept by my grandmother, Martha Jones, partly as an outlet for market-garden and farm produce from Witlow Farm (now a housing estate) where my mother's father, John Jones, farmed. A gardener in his younger days, he and my grandmother made their first home, when they married in 1875, on Caldey Island where my grandfather was a gardener. Now, a century later, that same shop is owned by the monks of Caldey who use it as an outlet for the world-famous perfume which they make on the island.

103   Bertie Howells (left) and his men, 1927.

56

104   Bill Frost.

Of all the harbour characters, however, none will be better remembered than the harbour pilots, or 'hobblers' as they were known in former years. At one time they had been taken on board the old sailing ships to pilot them in over the Cefn Sidan bar to Burry Port and Llanelli. On these trips a pilot would have his bicycle on board and then ride back to Ferryside, cross by the ferry to Laugharne, and return to Saundersfoot along the coast road through Pendine and Amroth.

Right up to the end of the coal-exporting activities at Saundersfoot the pilots continued to bring the boats into the harbour and see them safely out to sea again. When David Darby had retired, Jack Childs and Ted Goring continued in the business and there was intense rivalry between them when a boat was sighted coming in round Monkstone.

105   Author's grandmother, c. 1900.

106   Caldey shop, 1976.

107   Jack Childs.

108   Ted Goring.

109 **Billy Williams on the Rosalind with David Darby and Ambrose Lilbourne (right).**

Rivalry was not something which was confined to the pilots, however. On the sands there was considerable unpleasantness amongst the cockle-pickers. For many years there had been an excellent bed of cockles all the way from the back of the harbour to Monkstone. The old superstition was that you must never quarrel over the cockles or they will go away. Perhaps it was the quarreling which drove the cockles away from Saundersfoot, but the heavy over-picking (some said deliberately) by the Laugharne cocklers was hardly of very much help. Whatever the reason, there were no more cockles until fresh beds were put down by the South Wales Sea Fisheries Committee after the last war.

110 Locals picking cockles during World War I.

111 Laugharne cockle-pickers at Saundersfoot.

These affairs apart, law and order were generally in the safe hands of a sergeant and constable. Few village policemen could ever have been better loved and respected than the late Mathias Lloyd Nicholas who was the sergeant at Saundersfoot from 1922-33. For five years his constable was Stanley Henton, another of life's characters, who on one occasion was known to turn out, in his policeman's uniform, to keep goal for the village football team when they were one short. Saundersfoot ceased to be a sergeant station in 1946. Now only one policeman is stationed there, but it could be erroneous to infer that this is because people are now twice as law-abiding or that there is only half as much crime. On the other hand, the lone constable does have the help of a much-harassed traffic warden, which is probably just as well in an age when equally harassed motorists trying to park are recognised as constituting the bulk of the real criminal class, especially from mid-July to the first week in September.

112 Sgt. Nicholas.

113 P.C. Henton.

114 Sgt. William Evans and P.C. Anthony Thomas,
     1907. P.C. Thomas eventually became Deputy
Chief Constable of Pembrokeshire.

115 1976 same place.

Throughout the years, as well as being the focal point of the trading activities, the harbour every August was the basis for staging a regatta. It was begun in the 1870's by the sports-loving Ranken Vickerman. His son, Charles, became a keen yachtsman and, as well as competing at many regattas round the coast, including Cowes, patronised the Saundersfoot event which for many years attracted some very fine visiting yachts. With its longshore sports, greasy pole and swimming races in the harbour, the event became very much an affair of the people, until the harbour became so packed with pleasure craft that by the 1960's the regatta had to be abandoned.

116   Saundersfoot life-saving club, 1913.

117   Saundersfoot Volunteer Training Corps, 1915.

118   Peace Day 1918.

119   Saundersfoot sailing boats, 1904.

120   C. H. Vickerman's the *Ranee*, 1909.

121   Longshore sports and regatta, 1908.

122 Longshore sports and regatta, 1908.

123 Longshore sports and regatta, 1908.

64

124　Longshore sports and regatta, 1909.

125　Saundersfoot regatta early 1900's.

126   Regatta 1912.

127   A visiting competitor, the *Zinita* of Penarth,
      1912.

128   The harbour, 1883.

129   The Front beach, c. 1898.

130   Harbour and Front beach 1976.

131   Jack Childs laying up his boat, the *Stella Maris*,
       formerly owned by the Benedictine monks of
       Caldey, c. 1928.

132   The harbour in the 1920's.

133   The harbour in the 1920's.

134 The harbour, 1976.

135 The harbour in the 1920's.

136 The harbour, c. 1944.

137 The harbour, 1976.

A development from the longshore sports was the annual athletic meeting which was held at first in France Field and later in Coppet Hall meadow where it achieved its greatest renown with athletics, cycle racing and horse racing. Prize money was good and, in 1932, in the depths of the depression, an unemployed man walked all the way from Swansea to run in the mile race, which he won, and then walked back to Swansea with the money. In the same year the third Lord Merthyr, who had just succeeded his father who died that year, gave permission for the use of the meadow for the sports but refused to allow bookmakers. Without the 'bookies' the horse racing

lost its interest for the committed and, without the horses, the event lost much of its attraction. Its decline can probably be traced to this date.

A less spectacular event, but one which was much looked forward to by the village children, was France Fair, held in May on Ascension Day. At one time it had been the custom for it to be opened by a man carried round on a plank who used to shout, 'This fair will be open for three days'. Stalls of all descriptions extended right up to where the Drill Hall now stands and with more stalls and a roundabout in France Field.

138 Saundersfoot sports.

139   Saundersfoot—cycle race in progress.

140   Saundersfoot sports.

By the 1920's France Fair had become an event for the children and was based mainly on Cambrian Terrace. Money to sponsor the event was raised by a door-to-door collection. The greatest indignity was to have to stand in a row on the Office wall on the corner by the Hean Castle Hotel, formerly named the Picton and in those years still known in the village by that name. Two of 'the committee' would then come along with a bath full of treacle and buns. A third member with a long toasting fork would pass each contestant up a treacle-sodden bun which had to be eaten before we were allowed to jump down and run round the office. The good runners tended to cram the lot into their mouths and take off. Those of us who couldn't run so well tended to enjoy the buns first and run afterwards. Either way we had a penny each for our trouble and thank you very much for making us laugh.

The origin of France Fair is not known but, when I was a boy, I was told that it had 'something to do with an old hermit who lived on Monkstone'.

Now, the professional travellers have always either ignored the possibility of anyone ever having lived on Monkstone or have categorically stated that there are no remains there. This has always puzzled me because, as a boy, I spent many hours up on Monkstone and there were certainly remains there then. Mary Curtis, whose book appeared in 1880, seems to have been more discerning for she said that it '. . . had, no doubt, a cell for a recluse'.

In the September of 1976 I walked with Collin Bowen, an old school friend, to Monkstone and, for the first time for many years, climbed up on the point. The old wall foundations are still to be seen, although the

141   France Fair 1920's.

Royal Commission on Ancient Monuments for Wales had no previous record of anything there.

Monkstone first appears under that name on Saxton's map of 1578. There was a monastic settlement on Caldey from 1131 to 1536 and it would have been quite in keeping with monastic practice of the time for there to have been a cell there. Equally, there is no reason why it could not have been inhabited by some recluse at some time or other subsequently.

There are, of course, other possibilities. The building, such as it was, may have been for use as a beacon store, which is perhaps unlikely in view of its position on the rock. It is doubtful whether it could have been used in conjunction with quarrying activities and it is hardly much more likely to have been used by lobster fishermen. Whatever its purpose it would be interesting for archaeologists to give it a little expert attention.

142   Old foundations on Monkstone, 1976.

143   The Elephant's Trunk—an interestingly shaped rock between Swallow Tree Bay and Johnny's Grove.

I am saying it was probably used as a monastic cell and if I am proved to be wrong I am nowhere near as wide of the mark as those who say there was never anything there at all.

Mention has already been made of the village football team. Before the first war there was, for a short time, a rugby team, but, after the war, Saundersfoot United F.C. came into being as the result of a merger between the association football team, which developed from this side, and a team called Saundersfoot Rovers who played on the sands. By the late 1920's this village soccer team had become a real power in Pembrokeshire football, probably reaching their peak in the years up to about 1931, in one season winning all four cups on offer in the county, and including victories over Pembroke Dock, a professional team playing in the Welsh League. In that and the following season they were able to call on the services of George Kemp-Welch, a grandson of General Sir George Greaves who lived at Netherwood. In addition to playing cricket for Warwickshire and being a double Cambridge blue he played football for England and the Corinthians and had also turned out for Aston Villa.

This distinguished player apart, the real strength of the team was in young men of the village who played all their football for Saundersfoot, except when, for domestic reasons which would require a long chapter in itself to relate, they turned out on the odd occasion for the deadly enemies of neighbouring Kilgetty with whom the feud was long and bitter.

The three 'boys from the chemist', Tom, Billy and Jack (Ginger) Griffiths would have been outstanding in any company, as would their two cousins Leslie (Chester) and Harold (Snowball) Read, grandsons of the shipbuilder. Chester and Len Hunt, both brilliant ball players, attracted considerable attention from English League clubs. An almost unbeatable defence with Bob Phelps in goal, brother Harry at

144   Saundersfoot Rovers, 1921.

145 Saundersfoot A.F.C., c. 1929.

146 Kilgetty A.F.C., 1925.

centre-half, flanked by Stanley Scourfield and Charlie Phillips at full-back, were all heroes in a side which included other names such as Charlie Cox, Teddy Poole, Jack Davies, Billy ('Twin') Griffiths and, in slightly earlier years, the Hodge Brothers, Stanley Ormond, Tommy Williams and Billy Williams who, as well as being the last driver of the *Rosalind*, had also driven the old Ford lorry for my father and, as a boy, I spent many happy hours with him. 'Bertie Howells' lorry' was, in fact, just about the first means of transport the team had for away matches until the rather more sophisticated charabanc came along.

Support for the team, probably because the crowds will always follow a winning team, was fanatical. Perhaps the joy at such success was some sort of subconscious reaction to the despair of the times as the depression culminated in the closing of the pit in 1930. The village team played in red and white stripes and I found myself following the fortunes of English League clubs who also played in red and white stripes. They included Southampton, Sheffield United, Sunderland and Stoke, all, like Saundersfoot, beginning with the letter S and there were a couple of others whose names escape me. It was an interesting statistic until I realised that all it meant was that there were several teams whose names began with the letter S who played in red and white stripes and I made up my mind early in life that statistics counted for little.

In 1927, when football fever was reaching its peak in Saundersfoot, Cardiff City won the F.A. cup and it left England for the only time in its history. The trophy and the Welsh F.A. cup came to the village on display. The complete absence of security would have horrified today's administrators and, for the payment of a penny, we were allowed to drink lemonade through a straw from the most famous cup in the world.

There were only sporadic attempts to raise a cricket team and at one time the ladies had a hockey team, whilst Roger Griffiths, with considerable enterprise, laid out a couple of tennis courts at Coppet Hall near the sandbanks.

147 Howard Prout leaves Bonville's Court colliery from the last shift, 1930.

Indoors, at the British Legion rooms, where H. L. Read had had his ship-yard, there was a billiard table, and there was also a billiard table at the Coffee Tavern which was an institution in itself and, like many other aspects of village life at the time, would rank a considerable chapter of its own in any complete history of Saundersfoot.

The Evelyn Coffee Tavern, named after Lady Evelyn Campbell who opened it, was built in 1886 at a cost of £400 raised by public subscription to provide the seamen with an alternative to the attractions of the many public houses. The good temperance cause was supported by nonconformists and quakers but, right from the start, was the cause of contention with accusations that the church members were seeking to control its management. Commercially it was a white elephant until it was let to John Davies, a Rhondda Valley miner who had been injured underground and become a billiard hall steward. A very fine player himself, the village boys owed much to him, and the Coffee Tavern became the meeting place. As well as being run as a shop the premises also housed the magistrate's court and to 'go up the steps of the Coffee Tavern' was an accepted and well understood term for anyone in trouble with the law.

148   Billy Griffiths with the F.A. Cup, 1927.

149   The tennis court Coppet Hall.

150 Saundersfoot male voice choir early 1920's.
Author's father standing 8th from left.

151 Saundersfoot Boy Scouts, 1921.

n the winter evenings the male voice choir practised here and, at an early age, we became familiar, hrough listening on the steps outside, with the tirring choruses of Comrades in Arms, Crossing the Plain, Martyrs in the Arena and the Jolly Roger. Perhaps it was inevitable, in such distinguished musical company, that the parrot in the shop should ing 'God Save the King' and then, when cracking on he top note, shout 'Oh, Lord!'

For all their poverty, the 1920's saw the impact of motorised transport on a considerable scale and, from then on, the rate of change was more spectacular than anything which could have been imagined by those who had lived through years when the building of even one house had been the subject of comment in the local paper, and the fact that the railway station was a couple of miles from the village began to matter less and less. Cars began to be accepted as horses gradually disappeared from the scene, tradesmen went in for vans and a bus service to Tenby was pioneered.

152 Saundersfoot Girl Guides.

153 Cambrian Terrace, c. 1905.

154 Cambrian Terrace, c. 1905.

155   Cambrian Terrace, c. 1905.

156   Cambrian Terrace, 1976.

157   Roger Griffiths with one of the first motor-bikes
       to come into the village, 1914.

158   Stanley Scourfield with Saundersfoot's first
       delivery van.

159 William Beddoe Snr. in Milford Terrace,
     c. 1905.

160 Saundersfoot station, 1914.

161 Johnnie Ormond's first 'bus and the author's
father's motor bike and sidecar.

162 Greens 'bus links up from Haverfordwest and
Narberth.

163 Railway Street, c. 1906.

164 Railway Street early 1920's.

165   The Strand, 1976.

The last Ship being built on the harbour in the 1860's.

For years, the only piped water supply to the village taps had come from a disused trial for coal near Griffithston Farm and was always inadequate so that there was great dependance on wells until the Narberth R.D.C. laid on a main supply from the Preseli area. The same period also saw the introduction of electric light to the village and civilisation had really arrived at last.

166   John Edwards water carrier.

In the years between the wars, perhaps nowhere could the change in standards have been much more evident than in the building trade. Although some houses were still being built of stone there were fewer men who could work with stone, bricks were far more common and the day of the concrete block was at hand. Mortar was still being made from slaked lime and best sand, and for plaster the lime was strengthened by the addition of horse-hair for building. Horses, too, were on the way out and, horse-hair being increasingly more difficult to come by, coarse grass was used instead until plaster board took over. Fine ash, from the culm ball fires of the cottages, which had for years been used for mixing with the lime, was, however, becoming less plentiful because this type of firing was also on the way out. Windows which had previously been made by resident carpenters were now factory produced and delivered to the site.

My father was particularly fortunate in some of the men working with him. Jack Griffiths, the carpenter, and Billy Richards the stonemason, were superlative craftsmen whose work was a by-word in the area.

For the first time in almost a hundred years a new hotel was built. It was the St. Brides Hotel, at the top of St. Brides Hill, on the site of the house of that name, where there had many years previously been a farm. My father had the job when the idea was merely to convert the old house and add on about ten bedrooms. When the work was nearing completion it was decided to have thirty bedrooms and it was realised that it would have been much better to have knocked the old house down in the first place and start from scratch. Thus what is currently known in the horrible jargon of the day as a complex began to grow.

Many good houses were built during these years and, on St. Brides Hill and elsewhere, there was considerable development which only came to an end with the outbreak of war in 1939. About the only building during the war years was a large canteen on the village green but this was burnt to the ground in 1941 and not rebuilt.

167   The Glen and St. Brides Hill, 1904.

168   St. Brides Hotel, 1935.

90

Throughout these years most of the hotels and boarding houses in the village were requisitioned by the military authorities, but the highlight was probably in the summer of 1943, when more than 100,000 troops took part in operation *Jantzen* in preparation for the invasion of Normandy the following year, and a strict curfew and security regulations were imposed on everyone throughout the whole of the area involved, which was that corner of Carmarthen Bay from Monkstone to Marros.

In the years which followed the war there began a period of development in which the planning authorities of the National Park allowed large-scale developers to change Saundersfoot out of all recognition from the seaside village it had once been to an amphitheatre in which a concrete jungle is overlooked by myriads of little boxes. Welsh dolls made in Japan are a particularly pleasing line in this new subsidiary of the Persian market.

In the 60's there was a song which was sung by Pete Seeger about,

'Little boxes, on the hillside,
Little boxes made of ticky-tacky,
Little boxes, little boxes, little boxes all the same'.

At one stage a somewhat witty member of the R.D.C. made a rather scathing reference on these lines. A firm of developers took serious exception to his remarks insofar as they were taken to apply to one of their particular sites and the councillor apologised, presumably mindful of the maxim, 'The greater the truth, the greater the libel'.

Acknowledgement of the worth of this sort of planning culminated in the award of the O.B.E. to the planning officer. The cynics thought that the new Saundersfoot would have been sufficient memorial in itself.

On the credit side, there are still many beautiful areas around Saundersfoot due to the consuming life-long interest of the third Lord Merthyr in reafforestation and for which posterity will have cause to be grateful. The result is a living memorial far more satisfying than things which are transient.

Let it be said, however, that there is now a far wider enjoyment of the material benefits of life than in the times, the passing of which so many people are apt to bemoan. And where there is poverty it is nothing like as widespread.

169   Operation *Jantzen* 1943. Model of coastal area.
       U.S. Army photo.

170 Landing exercises on Front beach. U.S. Army
photo.

171 Directing operations from the culvert at Coppet
Hall. U.S. Army photo.

Spiritually, the enrichment has not quite kept pace. Three of the chapels in the village have become mere covered-in timber yards peopled mainly by the ghosts of their founding fathers, whilst the fourth, the Bethany, where my mother taught in Sunday school, and in the manse of which I was born, has long since closed and been turned into flats for old people. For this give full credit to the now defunct Narberth R.D.C. It could so easily have become just another bingo hall. The Anglican church, of course, which serves the whole of St. Issell's parish is some way out of the village, but a Roman Catholic church was built in the village in the 1950's.

172 Bethany chapel, c. 1900.

173 The author's mother, c. 1901 (formerly Nelly Jones).

93

174   The Front beach, c. 1900.

175   The Front beach, 1976.

176 The Front beach, c. 1900.

177 The Front beach, 1976.

178   The village, c. 1890.

179   'Visiting celebrity' Kenneth Griffith deep in
       conversation with one of the older inhabitants,
       Osborne Evans, about their own families.

Amroth

Written as Amtrud in 1230, Amerath in 1338 and Amreth in 1525, the name has also appeared variously as Amra, Amerar, Amrith, Ambroth and Ambroath.

The original form of the word was probably Amrath, from the Welsh Am meaning around or about, and the Celtic Rath, meaning an earthen fort or mound. This particular mound was situated to the south of where Amroth church now stands. The ancient earthwork fortifications known as 'raths' were situated so as to command and defend any approach from the sea through a valley and the name Amrath applied originally only to the land immediately surrounding this area.

In mediaeval times, apart from tracts of forest in the area, there was the great moorland of Amroth with several plots of cultivated land which included the parishettes of Merrixton, Amrath and Eareweare (the site of the present Amroth Castle), a tract of flat ground near the sea where there was a mill.

About the middle of the 15th century, prior to the building of the present tower church, there were three churches in Amroth. One was near the present church and had been referred to in the *Book of Llandaff* as Llanrath, the *llan* being the original Welsh for land, or sacred enclosure, on which a church would usually eventually be built. There was a newly erected chapel attached to Eareweare and a little church in a field, known as Church Park, at Merrixton.

With the increase in population and the cultivation of hitherto wasteland there was inevitable confusion amongst those who sought to claim tithes and amongst those who were demanded to pay twice on the same land. The solution came with the building of one larger church (about 1490) in the centre of the parish and consolidating the smaller ecclesiastical divisions, or parishettes, into one ecclesiastical parish.

The old church name, Llanrath, signifying the sacred enclosure near the rath, now became obsolete because it was inappropriate, and the new church acquired the parish name.

For the administration of the Poor Law, however, the parish continued with its former two chief divisions until, under the Act of 1834, it became part of the Narberth Union. The divisions were known as East Side and West Side, the dividing line being the brook running down from Penybont to the village. Paupers resident on either side had to be supported by ratepayers living on that side, but the system ceased when the Act of 1834 came into force.

With the old Vestry Meeting, and with the Parish Council when it was formed in the 1890's, it was an invariable rule in the appointment of overseers for the poor that one should be selected from each side of the parish but, in 1912, the tradition was broken by the Parish Council who selected both overseers from the west side. Half a century later the same division and failure to agree were evident in the building of two halls, one for the village and one for the parish. (The author was chairman of the village hall.)

Almost coinciding with the Act of Union came the building of the new Turnpike road to Pembroke Dock and the name Merrixton came to refer only to a couple of farms. The area previously known as Merrixton Bottom, once the new road and bridge had been built through the village, found the old name being superseded by the name 'Stepaside'.

As far as the parishette of Earweare was concerned, it is of interest that the name was still in use by the oldest Welsh summer visitors until well on into the 19th century for that part of the beach opposite the Castle. The land from the Castle gate to Amroth Arms in the village was known as Croggan's Cliff and the rest of the village was the Burrows.

The name, the Burrows, already referred to in writing of the patches, is still often used by the older people and is derived from the fact that the area was originally land which was covered with sandbanks honeycombed by rabbit burrows. When the village became enlarged by the building of houses along Croggan's Cliff, and the building of Ebenezer Chapel in the 1860's, the name the Burrows, through no longer being applicable, began to die out. The houses on both sides of the brook began to be known as Amroth Village and eventually Amroth, so that the name Amrath which originally applied to the parishette lands around the rath has survived the other parishette names to become the name of the whole parish, displaced the old name Llanrath to become the name of the central parish church, and has also displaced the old names of Earweare and the Burrow to become Amroth as it is known today.

The name Croggan's Cliff was derived from the nickname, Croggans, given to the Welsh speaking visitors in the summer. The great event was Amroth Big Day which was held in August on the first Friday after Narberth horse fair. From an early hour country people from 'up the Welsh' would descend on the village in gambos, carts and traps with an assortment of boiled hams and cold meat for a great day at the seaside, known as the Big Wash, from the old Pembrokeshire term, 'to wash in the tide', meaning to bathe.

180   The chapel window at Amroth Castle. In good condition up to 1960 but badly damaged since.

181   Benjamin Rees—died 1870—who gave the land on which Ebenezer chapel was built.

It was always a point of honour as to who would be the first to arrive and then, in addition to the bathing and the picnics, there would be sports on the beach and an open air concert on the Castle green in the evening.

Over the years the nature of the day changed considerably. Visitors from the surrounding areas still came for the day, but the villagers began to play a bigger part with a carnival and sports in the Castle grounds. Now, with the latter given over to the demands of the ubiquitous caravan, the sports and even the carnival have gone, but the Women's Institute, who have taken over the Village Hall, usually have a 'bring and buy' in the afternoon and, up to this time (1977) the concert in the evening also remains.

Another custom of the times, long since discontinued was that of the Lammas house. These were tents formerly made in several places in Amroth by the young people on or about Lammas day (August 1st). The young men erected the tent with poles and boughs covered with fern, and the girls prepared a feast of cakes, tarts and dumplings.

The last Lammas house of any note in the Burrows area was in the Steps Hill, in the area of Steps Cottage, where Penglyn house now stands, and which gave its name to the quarry nearby. One of the boys from Stepaside set fire to this Lammas house when the feast was in full swing. About the same time (1869) a Lammas house was built at Staggers Hill, near Stepaside but, although several attempts were subsequently made by the children to keep the custom alive, it had virtually become extinct in Amroth by about 1872.

182   Big Day carnival in the 1930's.

183   Amroth Castle, c. 1938.

184   The same site 1976.

About twenty years prior to this there had been the last use of the wooden ladder (or *Cefn Pren*) in Amroth when an unfaithful husband, who lived at Craigyborrian, was carried round the parish in derision at the instigation of his enraged wife. Far from mending his ways, however, the husband, a Mr. Severn, eloped on the following day with the governess with whom he had been having the affair.

Effigies, however, were burnt in the parish on several occasions after this, the last being in October 1892.

Throughout the present century Amroth has frequently been in the news as the village threatened by the sea, to tell all of which would be a long story in itself. In spite of all the attention, however, rarely does much thought seem to have been given to the overall picture of what has been happening along the bay.

When the tide is coming in, the current can be seen to run from west to east as anyone will know who has bathed in a rough sea when the tide is flowing. Although safe they will find themselves finishing up some distance along the beach to the east of where they went in. Likewise the pull is towards the west when the tide is ebbing. The prevailing wind is from the south-west and so it will be readily appreciated that, when high winds combine with spring tides, not only does the exposed part of the bay receive a terrible battering, but there is a considerable one-way-only movement of flotsam and jetsam to the east.

The ballast brought into Saundersfoot harbour for years by the coal ships, and dumped on the beach from the pier, when it was not used for such purposes as the building of Railway Street, was gradually washed along the beach towards Amroth. The same thing happened to the thousands and thousands of tons of waste from the iron ore activities from the patches. Even today the effect can be seen with the build-up of stones caught by the protrusion of Black Rock opposite New Inn to the eastern extremity of Amroth beach. With the cessation of the coal trade and, more especially perhaps, the end of the iron ore waste, the effect of the tide has been to denude the defences previously thrown up by the sea for the protection of Amroth and carry them steadily eastwards to leave the village increasingly exposed.

It is sad now to look through old newspapers and read again of the idiot prevarication of the County Council of the day with their interminable discussions as to whether they, as the highway authority, should spend money protecting private property until the road was actually threatened.

185   Amroth, c. 1910.

186   Amroth, c. 1920.

187   Amroth, c. 1938.

102

188   Amroth, c. 1950.

189   Amroth, 1976.

In the autumn of 1931 there was a series of huge storms which did immense damage. My father had a contract to patch the wall at the eastern end of the village and a new road was cut over the hill between the end of the village and the Castle gate. At the other end Thomas Richards, who owned the post office and cottages nearby, spent more than £500 (a great sum for a private individual in those days) building a wall in what proved to be a vain attempt to protect his own property. This included what was known as the Burrows Hall which he built about 1930 and consisted of six garages with removable partitions between them. These garages were let to summer visitors at a shilling a night through the season and, in the winter as well as for Big Day concerts, the partitions were removed to be used as seating and staging for concerts, whist drives and kindred entertainments which preceded the euphoria of 'the telly'.

In an age of high values on seaside properties it is interesting to note that houses on the sea side of the road in Amroth, like those on the sea side of Railway Street in Saundersfoot, were all built facing the road and with their backs to the sea.

190   Thomas Richards' sea wall.

191   The storms of 1931.

192   After the storm of 1931. The house was pulled
      down for the road to be built higher on the cliff.

193   The storms of the 1950's.

194   The storms of the 1950's.

195 After the storms.

196 After the storms.

Eventually Thomas Richards pulled down his garages, the cottages were washed away, and so was Cliff Cottage which stood near the site of the present public convenience, so that the only building left for a few more precarious years was the old stable opposite Morfa which had years ago been a bakery.

When all these and Thomas Richards' wall had been sacrificed to the sea, even the Roads and Bridges Committee of the County Council were forced to act at last and, in the post-war years, at fantastically greater cost than would have been involved if the problem had been tackled in time, new sea defences were built.

When the new road was made over the hill from the eastern end of the village to the Castle gate it meant that the gardener's house had to be pulled down. This had been built originally to replace a cottage which had stood outside the Castle gate and which had been pulled down to make room for Lord Kylsant's car to turn in. Not long before this, in about 1906, the bridge had been built over New Inn 'lake' (in Pembrokeshire running water is invariably referred to as a lake) and my father worked there when learning his trade.

197   The remains of Cliff Cottage.

198　New Inn 'lake' and Amroth Castle beach, 1902.

199　The same site 1976.

There is perhaps no great history to Amroth Castle and such as there is has mostly been told elsewhere. Early in the 19th century it was owned by Captain Ackland who, every quarter when his pension arrived, engaged men to make good the sea defences with pitchings or big stones laid flat to break the force of the in-rushing waves. Many of these stones were exposed by the great storms of the early 1950's and so was a path of white pebbles which he had made when Nelson had come to stay there with Lady Hamilton. After Trafalgar Captain Ackland had a commemorative plaque made in the ceiling of the lounge.

In the latter half of the century it was established as an asylum and eventually was bought by Owen Phillips who subsequently became Lord Kylsant. It is sad, but true, that, as Shakespeare said, 'The evil that men do lives after them, The good is oft interred with their bones'.

Lord Kylsant was a good landlord and a kind man, but he is best remembered now for the twelve months term of imprisonment in 1931 which followed exposure of his part in the gigantic swindle of issuing a false prospectus in his capacity as chairman of the Royal Mail Steam Packet. Those who would try to excuse him say that what he did had been done before and has been done since. It is a line of thought appreciated not at all by the many local people who had invested in his company and lost their life savings.

His wife had delusions of grandeur. Servants were expected to retire backwards from her presence and the windows where the servants passed in view of the gardens had obscure glass put in them so that these common people should not gaze upon them. When this age had passed and Amroth Castle had become virtually derelict my people took it on a twenty-one year fully repairing lease in the 1930's to turn it into a guest-house and my father, with his own men, was able to restore it for much less than it would have cost anybody else. When war came and the place was requisitioned, the wreckage, with virtually no compensation, was wanton and heartbreaking.

Long before this, possibly hundreds of years, there had been a secret underground passage from the castle either to the beach or the mill. This tunnel was come upon accidentally in the 1930's when work was being done on the outbuildings but it was covered in by the army when the place was requisitioned and the latrines drained into it. I am probably the only person now alive to have been down this tunnel.

With Amroth, as with Saundersfoot and, indeed, all villages, there have been many characters of whom, because of pressures of space, it is impossible to write. Yet the name of none, if only because of his official position in the parish, will live longer than that of Richard (Dick) Absalom. A grandson of Richard Howells of Duncow Hill, after whom he was named, his mother was a sister to Ben Howells. Dick Absalom was a blacksmith at the Foundry at Wisemansbridge and in 1901 became Clerk to the Amroth Parish Council. For another fortyfour years he served in this capacity and, when the Foundry cosed, he continued to support himself by acting as rate and tax collector for the parish.

In later years I did a ten year stint as Clerk to the Amroth Parish Council and, when research was necessary, it was a never failing source of admiration to look back over the beautiful writing of one who had probably, in his time, felt privileged to walk miles to pay his penny or two to attend school at Longstone before Stepaside school was built and he was able to learn at the feet of the renowned Skidmore. His neat and concise hand-written minutes will remain as a fearful indictment of some of the slovenly scrabble which is the product of today's free and free-thinking so-called education.

For my own part I am grateful that I was taught to write in a village school. Even today, more than half a century later, when I find my writing growing untidy I get back to basic principles by closing my eyes for a moment and imagining once again Miss Maudie Simpson standing behind me, putting the shoulders just so, sitting that way on the chair and holding the pen like this. The result is almost unbelievable.

200   Lord Nelson commemorative plaque Amroth
Castle.

201   Dick Absalom.

Proposed by Absalom John
Seconded by Thos Thomas That in consequence of
the Narberth Rural District Council.
having declined to put the Amroth Cliff.
Road in proper repair for Vehicular
Traffic, as requested by this Parish meeting
this council now appeal to the County.
Council to have the said Highway
properly repaired, and desire, owing to
the danger, and very great inconvenience
caused to the district, through the road
having been so long neglected. that the
work be carried out with as little delay
as possible. And also that a copy of
this resolution and the resolution of
the Parish meeting be sent to. the
County Council.
          An Amendment

202   Extract from Amroth Parish Council minute
book of 1901.

Dick Absalom's first business entry in the minutes on becoming Clerk was in reference to the state of the old Cliff Road, which ran from just above Wisemansbridge, past Duncow Hill, to Amroth, where it emerged by the Steps quarry. For years the carts had gone that way when driving coal from Bonvilles Court to Amroth, Pendine and Laugharne, as well as going across the sands when the tide was out. In places there had been cliff falls above the patches. When I was a boy it was no longer safe to go that way with a horse-and-cart. Stupidity, it will be realised, has never been the sole prerogative of Dyfed and kindred authorities, and nothing was done.

Posterity has Dick Absalom's writing to say that the cliff road has not been used for other than a footpath for most of this century. Still standing in the gateway to one of the fields along the way is a stout iron gatepost, dragged there and put into position by John Williams of Tinkers Hill, many years ago, from Kilanow, where it had served as a post to a tollgate belonging to the Tavernspite Turnpike Trust and which somehow seemed to escape the depredations of the Rebecca Riots. The gate was also moved to the Cliff Road and, for many years, remained there on the original posts but, although the posts have survived, the gate has long since been replaced.

203   Saundersfoot village school c. 1927.
      Miss Maudie Simpson right. Author front row right.

112

Unlike Saundersfoot, Amroth was not renowned for its football team or for any other sporting prowess. For a short time in the late 1920's they ran a team called Amroth Seagulls and, in more recent years, I ran a team known as Amroth Juniors which served its purpose insofar as it found the village boys something to do. If nothing else it made up the number and enabled a Junior Division of the Pembrokeshire League to be formed and, a quarter of a century later, this continues to flourish.

204   Toll-gat post Cliff Road, 1976.

205   Amroth Seagulls 1920's.

206   Amroth Juniors, c. 1949.

Ten Players of Amroth Juniors, 1984.

114

Fairs

Reference has already been made to France Fair in Saundersfoot and to Amroth Big Day. In days gone by the roundabouts were always an indispensable adjunct to such occasions and, even when they were no longer a part of these particular events, had a place of their own at various times of the year in the rural programme.

As a general rule the various family outfits would all turn up at the famous Portfield Fair annually in Haverfordwest and then go their separate ways to the various village events. For years Tommy Hill was a regular at Stepaside Fair on Whit Monday and at Amroth for a spell in the summer to coincide with Big Day. He had one of the old hand-cranked roundabouts and one of my favourite stories will always be of the seriousness of the situation when a distracted mother came along shouting 'I wants Mary to put her to bed', to which a furiously-turning Tommy Hill replied, with considerable indignation, 'I can't stop her now, 'ooman, she's gwain like merry hell'.

Mrs. Attewell, with a similar outfit, for years was a regular visitor to the harbour at Saundersfoot.

Originally Studts used to come to Saundersfoot in the summer, but pride of place in my own affections must always go to Danters because, ever since I remember, they were a part of Saundersfoot in the summer where they set up their galloping horses year by year as surely as the swallows returned in spring. Over the years, until diminishing space and all sorts of tin-pot regulations made life too impossible for them, they put up their stalls on no fewer than seven different sites, including my grandfather's field at Witlow. One night every season they would give all their takings to a village charity.

My father and Sid Danter were big pals and every year my father would help out the show people with the loan of planks, if needed, or by driving casks of water. Recently, when looking for pictures in connection with this work, I called on them and found Minnie Danter still living in the family caravan with its plate

207   Stepaside Fair, c. 1925.

glass mirrors and beautifu carved mahogany.

A younger member of the clan seemed to be little impressed either by my presence or my request for pictures. Eventually he disappeared. Five minutes later he returned and said, 'Are you Bertie Howells' son?' I said, 'That's right', whereupon he disappeared again. In no more than minutes he was back with a bundle of pictures and said, 'Mam can't come out of her van these days, but will you call and see her before you go'.

The Danters, in turn, had a great affection for Saundersfoot. In the 1950's they had set up on Kingsmoor Common, near Kilgetty, prior to moving on to Saundersfoot. As it happened, a baby was due and, recognising the symptoms in the young mother Minnie Danter was determined that no niece or nephew of hers was to be born on Kingsmoor, where the gipsies camp. Alarm signals were sent to the medical profession in the area and nurse Cousins, the District Nurse, travelled in the caravan with the young mother. They were just in time for the baby girl to be born as the caravan pulled in to Brewery Meadow in Saundersfoot.

During the war, the building in Swansea, where Danter's galloping horses were stored, was bombed and the horses were stolen. Nothing, however, will ever remove the memory of them for those for whom they were one of the highlights of the year when all the world was young.

208   Mrs. Attewell.

209   Some of the Danter family.

210   Danters' galloping horses.

211   Danters in the Cambrian hotel paddock Saundersfoot.

Corn threshing in the Cambrian Paddock.

The submerged forest

Along the shore from Wisemansbridge to Marros, remains of a submerged forest can be seen. Towards Marros there is more to be seen and the trees and roots seem to be in a better state of preservation. Possibly this is because the beach at Marros is less accessible and, being less frequented over the years, has suffered less from the depredations of man as a souvenir hunter and in his struggle to survive.

The remains retain the appearance of wood but the structure has broken down and, as wood, it is useless so that it is best left where it is. Even so, walking sticks and other articles have been made from the occasional suitable wood over the years. Particularly in the areas of Wisemansbridge and Amroth the face of the remains has been changed by the cottagers who for centuries dug slime on the beach to mix with the culm for their ball fires.

212   Remains of submerged forest at Marros 1976.

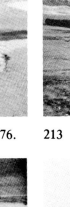

213   Remains of submerged forest at Marros 1976.

214   Remains of submerged forest at Marros 1976.

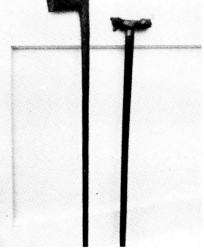

215   Walking sticks made from submerged forest remains at Amroth more than a century ago.

The trees of this forest, consisting mainly of oak, alder and willow, grew along the shores of the bay probably more than 4,000 years ago. Flints found over the years indicate that the inhabitants were of the later Stone Age and that, off Amroth, there was probably a factory. Eventually, they had to retreat to higher ground because there was, of course, no Roads and Bridges Committee in their time, and at Top Castle, overlooking Marros beach, there is a small camp which still shows quite clearly how man next lived in the area.

By this time, less than 4,000 B.C., man was keeping animals and tilling the soil. There is evidence of two terraces at Top Castle and, being more exposed on the landward side, but with the slope of the cliff below the outer bank being scarped to render the enclosure virtually inaccessible from the sea, it is clear that the defence was raised against enemies who would come from the sea.

Over the years, when digging for slime, the local people have come across skulls, bones and the antlers of red deer, the wild ox and other species long since extinct. Some found their way into museums, but others were cut up for making bone handles for knives. Ben Howells dug up a pair of antlers on the beach at Wisemansbridge but, although I can just remember seeing them when I was a boy, I have no idea what became of them.

The last wolf to be killed in Wales was said to be in the sixteenth century in Teague's Valley which is under the promontory fort of Top Castle. The last wolf, of course, is also said to have been killed in many other places so perhaps, like the proverbial cat, it had nine lives.

The derivation of the name, Teague's Valley, is not known, but Teague is the old Amroth area dialect term for an Irishman. And there were many itinerant Irish workers hereabouts at harvest time in former years.

216   Top Castle overlooking Marros beach.

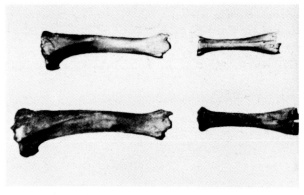

217   Bones of a *bos primigenius* dug up at Amroth in 1931 and given to the National Museum. This is believed to be the URUS referred to by Julius Caesar during his time in Germany but was probably extinct by the time of the Roman occupation of Britain.

120

Marros

The wild and lonely beach of Marros was for centuries the graveyard of stricken sailing ships as was the great stretch of Pendine sands just round the point, where Parry Thomas was killed in an attempt to break the land speed record in 1927, and where the hapless Jim and Amy Mollison took off for their much publicised Atlantic flight in 1933 from a spot very close to where the *Francis Beddoe* lay.

At one time it was said that most of the houses in Pendine had been built from the timber of ships wrecked in the area, and one building even took the name of the ship from the timbers of which it had been built. The wreckers of Pendine built an unenviable reputation for themselves. Very recently one of the older inhabitants told me that a skipper of one of the old sailing ships had once said to his father, 'I'd rather be cast up on the wildest coast of savage Africa than at Pendine'.

The last chance they had to indulge their trade was more than half-a-century ago when the *Treviga,* in 1923, was cast up at the normally delightful bay of Morfabychan, just round Ragwen point at the end of Marros sands. A Russian schooner from Riga, the *Treviga* was making her first trip from Trinidad to Cardiff with a cargo of pitch. The local paper account said that she had put in for shelter inside Caldey and that the skipper, Captain Jacobson, had said after the rescue he had been waiting for a tug. In actual fact the locals knew that the Saundersfoot pilot, Jack Childs, had gone out and offered to bring her in to Tenby harbour but that, rather than pay, Captain Jacobson had opted to ride out the storm at anchor. In the event the *Treviga* slipped her anchor in the night and was driven ashore at Morfabychan after the Tenby lifeboat had taken off the skipper, his wife and crew of seven. When the skipper arrived to see what was left of his ship he met a woman coming up the hill wearing his wife's fur coat. It can by imagined how much, or how little, there was left for the poor man to salvage.

218   Jim & Amy Mollison, 1933.

219   Remains of the *Rover* wrecked c. 1870's.

121

Marros Church is a building of great antiquity and, long before the wolf, the last in Wales or not, was killed in Teagues Valley, the people used to take refuge there from marauding wolves. Nearby was a school, which was opened in 1840 and which closed about 1875 when the new school was built at nearby Tremoilet. Until about this time there had been a thriving village at and around Marros, based on the activity of the many small quarries on Marros Mountain.

The most famous sculptor to work with Marros stone seems, undoubtedly, to have been Thomas Morris who lived for nearly fifty years, until his death in 1886, with his wife Jenny at Morfabychan. They died within a year of each other and were laid to rest side by side in Pendine churchyard.

Mary Curtis visited them in the 1870's when they were nearing the end of their days and wrote a picturesque account of the life they led.

220   Wreck of the *Treviga*, 1923.

221   Tom & Jenny Morris in the 1870's.

Tom Morris was born in 1804 and served his time as an apprentice with Rogers, the marble masons of Tenby, who built the Prince Consort Memorial on Castle Hill in Tenby in 1864. The stone for this came from Pwll quarry at Marros and it was with stone from this quarry that Tom Morris subsequently did some of his best work. He called it snowdrop marble. When polished it had a lustrous black surface flecked with white shells which, to the old craftsman's eye, had the appearance of snowdrops.

Specimens of his beautiful lettering and scrollwork are still to be found in neighbouring churchyards, as well as further afield at Amroth and other places, but he was also a musician of considerable ability upon the bass viol and, with ballads of his own composition, became known as the Bard of Morfabychan. George Borrow encountered him on his walking tour in 1857 with three of his music-loving neighbours at Beefs Park Farm, on the road from Marros to Amroth.

222   Tom & Jenny Morris's headstone Pendine.

223   Prince Consort Memorial, Tenby.

224   Tom Harries the day he finished Marros war
memorial, c. 1920. The original school is in the
background.

In another age there came another famous mason, although his talents tended more to the practical than the artistic. He was Thomas Harries (known as 'Tommy Harrie') who lived at Pwll Green alongside Pwll quarry. His own memorial is perhaps that which he built without charge in memory of the fallen of the first war at Marros. Help, too, was freely given, but the ex-servicemen were not allowed to help. The stones came from Pwll quarry but the three stones of the trilithon, with the cross-piece or lintel shaped like a coffin, were megaliths dragged from Garness, overlooking Marros beach, where there is a rich legacy of remains and circles which tell something of those who lived long ago and whose lives in places even yet impinge upon our own.

Is not this indeed the whole pattern of rural life?

225   Marros war memorial, 1976.

Glossary of local dialect

Since Edward Laws published his list of words in the dialect of Little England Beyond Wales other lists have also appeared from time to time. What is sometimes forgotten is that, within Little England Beyond Wales itself, the meaning of some words can vary from one area to another and, within these areas, some words have tended to live on or die out more so than in others.

There is no point in offering here a complete list, because those who are interested in the subject can find them elsewhere, but it may be of interest to include those words which have not previously found their way into print, especially as the list includes terms peculiar to the miners. Let it be emphasised that the list here offered is nothing more than a list of words not previously published and known to have been in common use in the Amroth and Saundersfoot area at the turn of the century with the meaning these words had in that area:

A

Aland	A colliery term signifying 'up to land'.
An	One—'big an' for 'big one'.
Apple-bird	The bullfinch.
Arrant	Right—'He had no arrant to do it'.

B

Baked	A bad case of constipation with farm animals.
Ball	The name of a game closely allied to hockey in which the goal is formed by a 'crick' or small stick fixed across two stones.
Balshag	A ragged or loosely attired person.
Bandy	The club used in the game of 'ball'.
Barriets	A fence made with wooden bars attached to posts with iron staples.
Barring	A colliery term for small timbers inserted horizontally behind larger upright posts and of the same meaning as the term 'lagging'.
Beam	Straw, or hay, twisted in a length for the purpose of tying sheaves.
Beat	To pare grassland.
Beatland	Land that has been pared with a breast plough and the parings burnt into ashes. Pronounced BETLAND and applied to any slow-burning fire of trash or garden waste.
Beelip	The beehive.
Beese	Cattle.
Berra	An article of child's clothing—substitute for petticoat.
Berrie	A rabbit's burrow.
Billy Ducker	The seabird known as the diver.
Billy Ho	Running frantically—'off like billy ho'.
Bloody Warriors	Wall flowers.
Bough	The wooden loop by which oxen were attached to the pole of a cart.

Brangel	A brazen-faced woman.
Branging	Burning intensely—'A branging fire'.
Brede	A colliery term for the breadth allotted to each stall.
Broomin-Broom	The shrub 'broom'.
Buckiboo	An imaginary person having a dragon-like form.
Budram	A kind of gruel made by steeping partially sifted oats in cold water for several days. The fermented water is then stirred, strained and the fluid part boiled until it becomes thicker, when it is sweetened with sugar or treacle and served.
Buff	A case used by colliers for carrying candles.
Bull-Toad	A fish about the size of a small trout which gives electric shocks.

C

Cabal	A row among several people.
Cambereen	A rope guide formerly used in sinking pits.
Cat	A short, double-pointed stick used by schoolboys in the game of Tip-cat, which, on being struck on one end rises into the air to again struck when it flies some distance away.
Chuck	The lower portion of a pig's head.
Clejjy	Sticky, as birdlime, or soft shoemaker's wax. Of a sticky nature.
Clog	A wooden fork for fixing round the head of a cow or pig to prevent it getting through hedges.
Clot	A clod.
Cluck	Sounding like cracked ware when struck with the knuckles.
Cluck	Broody, as a hen.

Cockalorum	The rod, or magic wand, used by charmers or faith healers.
Cockly-Nave	A term used at Amroth to denote the unearthly call made in the night by a bird formerly believed to be the bittern but now known almost certainly to have been the shearwater.
Cog	A colliery term for a support of the roof over the coal made out of sticks arranged crosswise in alternate layers.
Cows	Sea anemone—so called from the resemblance to cow teats.
Crampass	An iron firegrate supported on legs.
Creak	Hoarse; having a rough voice.
Cricks	Small sticks fixed across two stones in the game of 'ball'.
Crick-y-Barrin	The term used to denote a gateway or opening with walled pillars at each side, and one large crick, or barring, placed across to prevent cattle passing through.
Crinnacks	furze stems, or other small sticks, but more particularly applicable to furze, after being burned.
Crismal	A weakly child.
Croggans	A bye name for the Welsh people who visited the seashore in the summer.
Crogen	A shell fish; the scallop.
Crut	A small boy, but more especially one of about fourteen or fifteen.
Cursit	Mischievous.
Cutwyn	A windlass over a shallow pit.

D

Dabbs	Quits: being equal.
Dain	An interjection—'Oh, dain it all'.
Daize	A word used to express annoyance with oneself.
Dawl	A blow.
Dee	A colliery term for a piece of sheet iron, placed between rails so as to aid the transfer of a tram from one railroad to another at right angles to it.
Dill	The pine tree.
Dip-Side	A colliery term for the lower side.
Dog	A log of wood attached to a windlass over a pit on the opposite side of the beam so as to balance the tub or other box or skip when the latter is wound up.
Dorrix	Land covered with weeds or trash.
Drabble Tail	A slovenly dressed woman.
Dragmallin	A poor, hardworking woman.
Drapsy	A person who moves about lazily.
Druke	The handle of a windlass.
Dunfeddy	First reaping.
Dunstone	The strata lying immediately under the coal.

E

Eger	Acrid; very sour.
Ever	Ergot of rye.

F

Fall	Afterbirth of an animal.
Feak	Feeg; a whim; a freak.
Filty	Ugly.
Five Finger	The starfish.
Flew	A slap given on the side of a person's head.
Flugaries	Vagaries.
Floit	A flighty person.
Foot It	A game very similar to 'Leap Frog' in which boys give astride leaps over the backs of other boys in a bend.
Forehead	A colliery term for the face of the coal stalls.
Frath	Bold.
Frit	A small person or thing.

G

Gabbs	Iron catches which drop in automatically under a pit cage to prevent it falling back into the pit. Also conically formed rails at the edge of a 'spoor' or iron floor to guide a tram towards the rails.
Gane	A narrow trench.
Gedge	An interjection used to express obnoxiousness to the taste.
Gerts	Oats with the hulls off.
Gin	A type of capstan moved round by horse power, and used for winding at collieries before the days of steam power. It was something similar to the horse threshing machine.
Girt	A colliery term for a holiday.
Glob	To conglomerate.
Gob	A colliery term for a dry wall.
Gorral	A gormandizer. Gorral guts—greedy; 'skadly'.
Griskin	Slices of unsalted lean pork cut suitably for frying.
Gullack	To drink gluttonously.
Gunk, Gunkal	A small ravine; a natural trench worn deeply by water.

H

Hamtucks	The iron or brass fittings on a horse's collar to which the traces attached.
Harvest Bumps	Heat bumps; a kind of rash produced by heat.

Hasty Pudding	A kind of gruel made out of barley meal instead of oatmeal, with sugar or treacle added.
Hau Hau	Words used in driving cattle away.
Hen	A spiritless or cowardly person.
Hiss	To set a dog on.
Hisso	A word used in driving a pig away.
Hoaking	To visit or hang on others for maintenance.
Hoch	Warped ; crooked.
Hucks	Looped cords used for tying a pig's legs when it is killed on a block.
Hud	A conical formed covering of earth over potatoes.
Hurts	The fruit of the whortleberry.

J

Jander	Frog spawn.

K

Kambrell	A strong cross stick used for attaching a rope in hanging slaughtered animals.
Karp	'To put on side' or 'crack the jaw'.
Kensal	The seed pod of the wild rose.
Kor	A partition in a cattle shed fixed between the wall and the heads of cattle with a passage between to allow fodder being taken to the animals.
Kroker	A person broken down either in health or business.

L

Laggings	A colliery term for small poles placed horizontally inside the larger upright timbers.
Lamfa Lane	Behind the scenes.
Landside	A colliery term for the upperside.
Leer	Empty or hungry. Also a colliery term applied to an empty truck.

M

Mandrel	A pick axe.
Mannish	Proud ; said of boys who are 'too big for their boots'.
Maw	Inclination for food—'To maw for food'.
Middling	Fairly well, as distinct from some areas where it means not very well.
Mine	Iron ore.
Molla	Earth, or mould, of a brittle nature and free from clayiness. Moll earth is the result of being continually mixed with ashes.

Money Wedding	A wedding at which a dinner is given to guests who contribute money or other gifts. The couple are escorted to church by a large number of friends headed by an instrumentalist, usually a violinist or accordionist.
Mute	The hinny ; the product of a stallion and an ass.

N

Nacky	Handy. Clever with the hands. Inventive.
Nado	An animal stunted in growth or weakly.
Narch	Odd-mannered ; Eccentric.
No Shape	Bad in any way.
Nurr	A small insignificant person.

O

Oar Weed	A kind of seaweed which grows on rocks covered by the tides, with leaves shaped like an oar.

P

Paik Paik	The distant call to a pig.
Park	A field.
Patches	Where iron ore was dug.
Peeks Peeks	The coaxing near call for a pig.
Pigs Nut	A pressing of the thumbs behind someone's ears to inflict pain.
Pin	A seam of iron ore.
Pitchers	Small, young whitethorns.
Pleat	A small layer of old hay.
Ploppy	Very soft.
Poll	To go off with a young man's sweetheart but with her consent.
Poll	To chip off slate or shale from iron ore.
Poller	A person who polls iron ore.
Porr	To eat gluttonously.
Pottery	Feeble in health.
Progue	To probe or poke.
Prwy	The cow call.
Pulk	A pool, especially on the seashore.

R

Rammas	Rote ; The name applied to the long speech made by the Lavier on his return to the wedding house having been away all day inviting guests to a money wedding. The invitation to the guests was also in the form of a rammas. Hence any long, rambling story.
Rang-al	A very tall person.

Red Cow	The insect known as the ladybird or lady cow.
Ribe	A kind of strap used for putting a fine edge on scythes.
Riggel	A groove.
Rochl	The death rattle.
Rodni	A man or boy who strolls about when he should be at work.
Rottle	Wholly; entirely; completely. person gone insane is said to be 'rottle dull'.
Rowy	Streaky, as in bacon.
Runcoal	Soft gaseous coal, as distinct from anthracite.

S

Sangle	A term formerly used among gleaners for a handful of gleaned wheat straw.
Scanch	A lift, or step of strata worked downwards in quarrying.
Scarbut	Flesh of the fish called ray or thornback.
Scot	Money collected by the taler among the guests at a money wedding (after the gifts were received) and spent as desired by the giver either in providing cakes or drink for himself or others.
Scrade	A thin, scraggy looking man or woman.
Seed	Seen; past tense of see, 'I seed him coming'.
Shilboldien	A torch made of fat, lard, etc.
Shocky	Shaky through nervousness.
S.K.	A link in the form of an S used in repairing broken chains. The link is attached and the ends are then closed with a hammer.
Skadly	Very greedy.
Skadly Pluck	The act of throwing pence, sweets, nuts, etc. among a crowd of children and each child quickly grabs as many as possible.
Skirp of rain	A very short shower of rain.
Skred	To chop into small pieces.
Slabback	A dirty, slovenly person.
Slaps	Old shoes nearly worn out.
Slash	A kind of inferior coal sometimes known as 'smelting'.
Slatch	A lump or mass of coal not lying in the usual form of a vein or seam. 'Slash' or 'smelting' is mostly found in the form of a slatch.
Slough	A rut or trench made by a cartwheel.
Smelting	See 'slash'.
Smut	A kind of very soft anthracite found in the cliffs where the regular vein outcrops.
Sneag	Mucus from the nose. Anything slimy.
Snib	A young man who lacks confidence or is bashful.
Snut	A short piece of candle.
So-leaf	Same as 'as leaf'—'I so-leaf have one as the other'.
Spoor	A floor made of cast ron plates.
Spril	A boy or girl grown very tall and thin.
Stall	A colliery term denoting the part of the workings allotted to two or more coal diggers.

Stife	Dust. Generally used to denote dust on the roads.
String	A small narrow seam of coal.
Style	A colliery term for steep or sloping.
Sucky	Very sick in love with much fondling. A sucky calf.

T

Talking tree	An arrangement at old collieries in the form of a lorry on wheels, that was run in under the cage or skip, or tram, and then drawn out with the detached skip on it, when the coal was tripped some distance away, and the skip returned to the shaft again ready for lowering, when the pit rope was attached and the taking tree removed.
Taler	The best man at a money wedding. His duties were to do all waiting necessary, such as carrying beer and cakes and also to keep the people merry with stirring tales—hence the name.
Tantany fire	Erysipelas.
Tare	Brazen faced.
Teague	An Irishman (in contempt).
Tech	(Welsh pronunciation) Hoarse, asthmatical.
Tizzicky	Wheezy. Breathing hard.
Top	To snuff a candle with the fingers.
Toust	A blow to the side of the head.
Trek	'To make treks', to start travelling. To move on.
Trippet	A stool wholly made with boards.

W

Whech	To laugh in a giggling manner.
Whirry	A windlass in action. Probably so called from the whirring sound. The windlass was sometimes known as a 'beam and druke'.
Wilg	The willow tree.
Windroad	A colliery term for an airway.
Withy	The honeysuckle or woodbine.
Wran or Wron	The wren. 'Cursed be the man who kills a robin or a wran'.
Wyer	To work sharply—'I must wyer in now'.

Y

Yamming	Longing. Anxious to acquire. 'Yamming for food'.
Yawk	To clear the throat of phlegm.
Yerrack	The earwig.

Z

Zappy	A silly person.
Zawny	A lazy person.

Index

A

Absalom, Richard, 110, 112
Ackland, Capt., 110
Advance, 7
Africa, 121
Amroth, 1, 25, 34-37, 39, 57, 97-114, 119, 120, 123, 126
    Arms, 97
    Big Day, 98, 108, 115
    Burrows Hall, 104
    Castle, 97, 99, 110
    Juniors F.C., 112
    Parish Council, 97, 110
    Post Office, 104
    Seagulls F.C., 112
    Village Hall, 97, 99
    Women's Institute, 99
Anthracite, 9
Armour, 41
Aston Villa, 76
Attewell, Mrs., 115

B

Balls, 25, 89, 119
Bancroft, Rev. George, 33
Barbecue, 54
Basin, the, 29, 31
Beddoe, Francis, 7
Beefs Park, 123
Begelly, 39
Bethany, 33, 54, 93
Bethesda, 33
Betjeman, John, 34
Black Rock, 101
Black Walk, 1
Blaencilgoed, 36
'Boers', 41
Boer War, 41
Bonvilles Court, 1, 10, 14, 16, 23, 31, 33, 41, 112
Borrow, George, 123
Bowen, Collin, 74
Brandy Back, 49
Brewery, 33
Brewery Meadow, 116
British Legion, 78
Brodrick, St. John, 56
Bulldog, 14
Burrows, the, 35, 97, 98, 99
Burry Port, 57

C

Caldey Island, 56, 75, 121
Cambrian, 39
Cambrian Terrace, 74
Campbell, Lady Evelyn, 78
Cardiff, 121
Cardiff City F.C., 78
Carmarthen Bay, 89
Castle Ely, 39
Cefn Sidan, 57
Cheshire, 6
Childs, Jack, 57, 121
Cliff Cottage, 108
Cliff Road, 112
Clom, 23
Coal, 1, 4, 23, 41, 57
Cockles, 58
Coffee Tavern, 79
Combe Martin, 7
Coppet Hall, 1, 10, 72, 78
Cornish Lass, 23
Corinthians, 76
Cousins, Nurse, 116
Cowes, 61
Cox, Charlie, 78
Craigyborrian, 101
Cresselly, 25
Crickdam, 35, 37
Croggans Cliff, 97, 98
Culm, 23, 25, 36, 89, 119
Curtis, Mary, 74, 122

D

Danters, 115, 116
Darby, David, 7
David (Foundry), 45
Davies, Jack (footballer), 78
    John (Coffee Tavern), 78
    John ('Cap'n Jack'), 7, 56
Dayton, 54
Devil's Den, 49
Doss house, 33
Drill Hall, 34, 72
Dublin, 9
Duncow Hill, 1, 39, 45, 110, 112
Dunn, Jim, 7
Dyfed, 112

E

Earmere, 97, 98
East Anglia, 9
Ebenezer chapel, 98
Evans, Ann, 50
    Walter, 49, 50

F

F.A. cup, 78
Ferryside, 57
France Fair, 72, 74, 115
France Field, 72
Francis Beddoe, 7, 121
Frost, Bill, 54, 56

G

Gangrel, the, 49
Garness, 125
Gaunt, Thomas, 34
General Strike, 54
Globe, the, 26
Goring, Ted, 57
Graham, W. J., 7
Great Western Railway, 29
Greaves, General Sir George, 76
Griffiths, A. D., 25, 26
    Billy ('Chemist'), 76
    Billy ('Twin'), 78
    Edmund, 50
    Jack ('Ginger'), 76
    Jack (Carpenter), 89
    Roger, 78
    Tom (Dr.), 76
Griffithston Farm, 89
Grove ironworks, 34, 37, 41, 43, 50
    limekilns, 41
    pit, 36, 41, 50
Guinness, 125

H

Hamilton, Lady, 110
Harries, Thomas, 125
Harvey, E. J., 31
Haverfordwest, 115
Hean Castle, 6, 31, 33, 45
Hean Castle Hotel, 74
Henton, P.C., 59

Heronsmill, 49, 50
Hill, Tommy, 115
Hilling, John, 33
Hobbs Point, 39
Hodge Brothers, 78
Howells, Ben, 39, 110, 120
    Bertie, 78, 116
    George, 4
    Richard, 1, 4, 37, 39, 110
Hunt, Len, 76
Hunter-Dunn, Dr., 34
    Joan, 34

I

Incline, 14, 29
Ireland, 9
Irish workers, 120
Iron ore, 1, 34, 36, 37, 101

J

Jacobson, Captain, 121
Jantzen, 89
Jeffreston, 25
Jersey, 7
John, Bob, 35
Jones, John, 56
    Martha, 56
    Nelly, 93

K

Kemp-Welch, George, 76
Kent, 9
Kilanow, 112
Kilgetty, 53
Kilgetty F.C., 76
Kilgetty pit, 43
Kingsmoor Common, 25, 116
Kylsant, Lord, 108

L

Lady of the Isles, 7, 25, 56
Lammas, 99
Laugharne, 57, 58, 112
Laws, Edward, 126
Lewis, Sir William Thomas, 31
Lime, 1, 36, 89
Llanelli, 57
Llanstephan, 35

Lloyd, Jimmy, 50
  William, 35
Longstone, 110
Loveston, 1
Lower Level, 39, 41, 49
Ludchurch, 36

M

Marros, 89, 119, 120, 121-5
Mary Jane Lewis, 23
Mathias, Bentley, 26
  Thomas, 26
Merrixton, 97
Merthyr, Lord, 31, 72, 91
Milford, Lord, 4, 6
Milford Arms, 39
Mine, 35
Miners' Arms, 36
Miners' Express, 41
Mistley, 9
Mollison, Amy, 121
  Jim, 121
Monkstone, 57, 58, 74, 75, 91
Morfa, 108
Morfabychan, 121, 123
Morris, Mrs. (Jubilee House), 25, 29
  Billy, 26
  Jenny, 122
  Thomas (Heronsmill), 49
  Thomas (Morfabychan), 122, 123
Mountnessing, 31

N

Narberth R.D.C., 89, 91, 93
  Union, 97
National Park, 91
Nelson, Lord, 110
Netherwood, 76
New Alus, 45
New Hayes Pit, 4
New Inn, 101, 108
Nicholas, Sergeant, 59
Normandy, 91

O

Office, the, 54, 74
Ormond, Stanley, 78

P

Pan, the, 36
Patches, 34-7, 101, 112
Pelecwm Slack, 49
Pembrey, 34
Pembroke Dock, 39, 97
Pembroke Dock F.C., 75
Pembrokeshire County Council, 101, 103
Pembrokeshire League, 112
Pendine, 7, 57, 112, 121, 122
Penglyn, 99
Penybont, 39, 97
Phelps, Bob, 76
  Harry, 76
Philipps, Owen, 110
Phillips, Charlie, 78
Picton, the, 74
Pollers, 36
Poole, Teddy, 78
Poor Law, 97
Portfield Fair, 115
Port Talbot, 37
Preseli, 89
Prince Consort Memorial, 123
Pwll, 123, 125

R

Ragwen, 121
Railway Street, 7, 34, 101, 104
Read, H. L., 7, 79
  Harold, 76
  Leslie, 76
  Reggie, 31
Reading, 7
Rebecca Riots, 112
Riga, 121
Richards, Billy, 89
  Thomas, 104, 108
Roads & Bridges Committee, 108, 120
Roblin, Tom, 25, 29
Rogers (marble masons), 123
Rollin, 49
Rosalind, 14, 23, 41, 43, 78
Rosehill, 49
Royal Commission on Ancient Monuments for Wales, 75
Royal Commission on Land, 1893, 33
Royal Mail Steam Packet, 110
Royal Yacht, 9
Runcorn, 6
Rushyland, 49

S

Santos-Dumont, Alberto, 54
Saundersfoot harbour, 1, 14, 23, 25, 29, 37, 41, 53, 56, 57, 61, 101, 115
    male voice choir, 54, 81
    Rovers, 76
    United F.C., 76, 78
Saxton, 75
Scourfield, Stanley, 78
Seeger, Pete, 91
Severn, Mr., 101
Sheffield United, 78
Simpson, Maudie, 110
Skidmore, 110
Slash, 23
Slater's Directory, 1
Snape, 9
Southampton, 78
South Wales Sea Fisheries Committee, 58
Staggers Hill, 99
Stepaside, 1, 4, 10, 14, 23, 34-48, 53, 97, 99, 110
    canal, 4
    fair, 115
Steps Hill, 99
Steps Quarry, 99, 112
Stoke City, 78
Stokes, Thomas, 45
Stone Age, 120
Studts, 115
Strand, the, 34
Sunderland, 78
St. Brides Hill, 31, 54, 89
St. Brides Hotel, 89
St. Issell's House, 31
St. Issell's Parish Council, 33
Swallow Tree, 1
Swansea, 72

T

Tavernspite Turnpike Trust, 112
Teague's Valley, 120, 122
Templeton, 53
Tenby, 1, 81, 123
Thoby Priory, 31
Thomas Chapel, 4, 10, 14
Thomas, Parry, 121
Tinker's Hill, 112
Tit Bits, 33
Top Castle, 120
Trafalgar, 110

Tramps, 33
Tremoilet, 122
Trinidad, 121
Triviga, 121
Turnpike road, 97

U

Underfoot Hill, 49

V

Verbena, 7
Vestry meeting, 97
Vickerman, Charles H. R., 7, 31, 61
    C. Ranken, 6, 7, 31, 33, 61
    Eleanor, 7, 31
    J. F., 31
    John, 6
    Rosalind, 14, 31
Victoria, Queen, 9
Visitors, 1, 33, 53-4

W

White Leys, 35
William the Conqueror, 31
Williams, Billy, 78
    John, 112
    Tommy, 78
Wisemansbridge, 1, 4, 10, 34-48, 110, 112, 119
Whitlow Farm, 56, 115
Woodcock, 7
Wood Level, 23
Woodside, 45, 110
Wright, Orville, 54